A WORD FROM THE AUTHOR...

Life's not really divided up into neat little topics.
Neither is this book.

I've included material because it makes a good story,
because facts are often weirder than fiction, and because
sometimes you need background material to truly
appreciate how bizarre life can be. Some of these
stories have nothing at all to do with explosions,
but I thought you'd enjoy them anyway.

BiG BANGS

BEVERLEY MacDONALD

CARTOONS BY **ANDREW WELDON**

ALLEN & UNWIN

This South Asian Edition Published in 2004

Allen & Unwin
9 Atchison Street
St Leonards NSW 2065
Australia
Phone: (61 2) 8425 0100
Fax: (61 2) 9906 2218
Email: frontdesk@allen-unwin.com.au
Web: . http://www.allenandunwin.com

National Library of Australia
Cataloguing-in-Publication entry:

MacDonald, Beverley.

  Big bangs.

  ISBN 1 86508 354 2.

  1. Volcanoes – Juvenile literature. 2. Explosives – Juvenile literature. 3. Natural
  disasters – Juvenile literature. 4. Outer space – Juvenile literature. I. Weldon,
  Andrew, 1971-. II. Title.

500.835

This edition is for sale in India, Bangladesh, Pakistan, Sri Lanka & Nepal only.
Not for export elsewhere.

Designed and typeset by Sandra Nobes in 12pt Rotis Serif
Printed and bound in India by Replika Press Pvt. Ltd., Kundli 131 028

? ? ?

This book is for my son, Luke, a champion.

And for my brother, Chris, who shares my passion for history and patiently answered my stupid questions. Any mistakes are mine, not his.

TIMELINE
STARTS
HERE

15 billion
years ago
Big Bang

contents

JUST IMAGINE...

You are on your way to school. You carry your lunch box and schoolbooks. It seems like a perfectly ordinary morning. You meet up with your friends and walk together across the concrete bridge. Perhaps you talk about what you're going to do when you leave school. It seems just like every other morning, but suddenly in the distance you hear a siren. At first, you're not worried. It's an air-raid siren and it might be just a drill. You look up into the sky to see a single plane flying high overhead, so high you cannot hear the sound.

But you watch as a tiny black speck falls away from the plane, just for a second. And then you see a fireball explode in the air above the city, a huge fireball that continues to expand. It's coming towards you. Another few seconds pass and the sound reaches you – a terrible roar, the loudest sound you've ever heard. You fall to your knees as the heat blast ignites the city around you. But this time you're lucky. You knelt behind a concrete pillar on the bridge. Your school friends were not so lucky. All that is left are their shadows burnt into the concrete bridge. They have been vaporised.

And around you the firestorm begins, as every combustible material bursts into flame, sucking oxygen into the growing holocaust of fire.

Fiction? If only it was. This happened to many school children in Hiroshima on 6 August 1945 when the first atomic bomb to be used on a city was dropped at the end of World War II.

In the museum in Hiroshima you can still see the lunchbox, but the contents have been turned into charcoal – as was the young schoolboy. He was burnt beyond recognition: his mother could identify only the lunchbox.

You are a peasant farmer in Mexico. Every morning you make the dusty trek to your cornfields. You carry your hoe, as you do every morning.

At lunchtime you will stop to roast corncobs over a fire. But this particular morning the birds and animals are silent.

When you arrive at your field, you notice an odd crack in the ground and, even as you look, it grows larger and longer. Strange. You put down your hoe and stare.

Suddenly the earth begins to shake. It takes you a second to realise it's an earthquake. It's not the first time you've felt earth tremors, but the crack in the ground is getting bigger. Steam and gas begin to spurt from the crack. Now it's time to drop your hoe and run, as hot, glowing lava shoots high into the air. Frightened, but also curious, you stop and watch from a safe distance as lava and steam pour from the earth.

Within a week there is a small hill of cooling lava 150 metres high in the middle of what is left of your cornfield.

You've just witnessed the birth of a volcano.

Fiction? No. This really happened outside a little village called Paricutin in Mexico in 1943. The volcano remained active for nine years, by which time it was 2,770 metres high.

It's a cold winter's day. A brisk breeze scatters the few clouds in an otherwise clear sky. It rained earlier this morning and the streets are just drying out. A few people are about, working in their gardens, driving their cars. It's just a typical day in a small town...

As you stroll down the street, a small pink object in the gutter catches your eye. Are you seeing things? Another pink shape falls directly in front of you. You blink again. The pink shape moves. It has eyes and legs. It hops! It's a frog, a tiny pink frog. Now, you've heard the expression raining cats and dogs, but this is ridiculous.

All around you, hundreds and hundreds of tiny pink frogs are falling from the sky. They are collecting in the gutters, covering the footpaths. Are you going mad? Perhaps you shouldn't have eaten that pizza last night – this must be a really weird dream. But around you other pedestrians are also stopping to stare, open-mouthed, at the tiny hopping creatures. People are getting out of their cars, staring out their windows at the impossible spectacle. Children are starting to collect the tiny frogs by the bucket load.

Fiction?

No, this really happened in an English town, Cirencester, in February 1988. The Gloucester Trust for Nature Conservation investigated, concluding the frogs were native to the Sahara desert and had been 'airlifted' by a freak wind all the way from the Sahara to England. And why were they pink? They'd been stained by the red desert sand, explained the Trust.

MAKING BIG BANGS

Starting With A Bang

Explosions occur when huge amounts of energy are released in a short time in a confined space. The very first 'big bang' may have created the cosmos. Relatively smaller explosions created the galaxies and stars. On Earth, natural explosions such as volcanoes, earthquakes and thunderstorms helped create the surface of our planet and atmosphere.

Explosions aren't all bad, but...

A Word Of Warning

...all explosions are dangerous, whether natural or man-made. Sure, they can be exciting too, but every year many people are maimed and killed by explosions.

Of course, these things only happen to other people. Wrong! Treat every explosion as though it is deadly. Every gun could be loaded. Every lightning bolt has to strike somewhere. Don't let it be you!

In 1978 an American rock musician, Terry Kath, was fooling around with a gun. He thought he'd play Russian roulette, spinning the bullet chambers before he put the gun to his head and pulled the trigger. His friends were alarmed. 'Don't worry, it's not loaded,' Terry reassured them just before he pulled the trigger and blew off his head. Terry was wrong, the gun was loaded.

Always try to keep a safe distance between yourself and any explosion.

Unfortunately, some explosions are so big there is no safe distance. Nobody can give you any practical advice about where to stand when the sun finally explodes.

winneRs anD LoseRs

The history of the human race is, to some extent, the history of winners and losers. Humans first fought each other using brute strength, and the biggest and strongest generally won. One day someone threw a rock or a lump of wood, and mankind began the arms race – the race for superior weapons. Clubs, spears, bows and arrows, swords – the weapons became more and more sophisticated, until finally someone stumbled on the formula for gunpowder.

Of course, there have been historical moments of individual bravery, self-sacrifice, courage, wisdom and discovery, but the story of the human race is also the story of warfare, and people's capacity to be barbaric to each other.

A BRIEF HISTORY OF THE WORLD (CONDENSED)

BURNING THE GUY

On 5 November each year, people in England celebrate Guy Fawkes night. In many towns and suburbs, combustible material is collected into a bonfire and set alight. Everyone brings crackers, catherine-wheels, skyrockets and Roman candles. The highlight of the evening is the burning of the 'guy' (a figure made from old clothes and stuffed with paper and rags). It can be very exciting – except occasionally someone holds onto a cracker for too long, or a skyrocket goes astray and explodes into the crowd instead of into the air. Fireworks can be dangerous and people can be seriously hurt, even innocent bystanders just watching the spectacular show.

What is Guy Fawkes night? Guy Fawkes was a real person. He lived in England in the seventeenth century, and he was a member of the 'Gunpowder Plot'.

In Europe in the early 1600s, the struggle for power between Catholics and Protestants was deadly serious. The new English king, James I, was a Protestant, and some of the Catholics decided to blow up parliament, and the king. The Catholic conspirators discovered an old cellar beneath the Palace of Westminister (the English House of Parliament) and stacked it with gunpowder – thirty-six barrels of gunpowder.

But someone betrayed the conspirators, and on 5 November 1605, Guy Fawkes was caught red-handed in the cellar, just as he was about to set fire to the barrels of gunpowder. Guy Fawkes was tortured on the rack until he confessed the names of the other members of the Gunpowder Plot. He was promptly executed along with seven other conspirators.

Guy Fawkes Day is still celebrated in England. Most people celebrate the fact that parliament was saved, but others cheer Guy Fawkes's attempt to do away with the government. It all depends which side you're on.

THE TORTURE RACK

The rack was a medieval instrument of torture used to extract confessions of guilt. The torture rack consisted of a strong wooden frame fitted with a large roller at each end. The prisoner was laid on the frame, ropes were tied to his ankles and wrists, and connected to the rollers. Then the prisoner was advised to confess everything. If he (or she) didn't, the rollers were turned until finally his arms and legs popped out of their sockets. The pain must have been excruciating, and at this point most people confessed to anything.

WHO WRITES HISTORY?

History is generally written by two sorts of people. First, people who can write! Many early cultures did not develop writing. Archaeological evidence such as paintings, carvings and architecture may give us some clues about how they lived or died, but we don't know what they thought about themselves and the world, because they left no written records. Often we only know about these people because of what *other* people wrote about them.

Which brings us to the second group of people who wrote history – the winners. The historians of ancient Rome wrote about the people and lands they conquered, but the people of ancient Britain did not have a written language. They passed on their history through oral tradition (storytelling). Unless someone wrote down these stories, they disappeared forever when the people died. We don't really know what the ancient Britons thought about the Romans. We do know they fought against Rome's invasion, and several times started bloody rebellions – all of them ultimately unsuccessful. But even the stories of these battles were written from the Roman point of view – the winners.

If we could ask Guy Fawkes to tell his side of the story, it would probably be completely different.

CALCULATING CENTURIES

There is no year zero. Year one is designated as the year Christ was born – AD 1. AD stands for *Anno Domini* (Year of Our Lord) – the Christian era. The year 1 BC is one year Before Christ was born.

Years AD 1 to AD 100 are called the first century. Likewise, years AD 101 to AD 200 are called the second century. You can calculate this quickly: if it is the seventeenth century, the numerals will be one less, that is 1601–1700 (roughly the 1600s). Another method is to remember that a century ends with the year of the same numeral. So, the thirteenth century will *end* with the year 1300, and the sixth century will *end* with the year 600. The year 2000 is the last year of the twentieth century. The twenty-first century starts with the year AD 2001.

Of course, this system of keeping track of time was not in use until many centuries after Christ was born. Previously it was common to date things by the reign of kings (or emperors, or Pharaohs etc.)

CATAPULTS
TO
CANNONS

THE SIEGE OF MASADA

It was dawn when Simon slipped out of bed, drew on his sandals, grabbed a woollen shawl against the cold air and unlatched the door. His mother was still asleep on the low bed beside the fire, but he knew she would soon rise to begin the never-ending chores of the day, and he intended to be gone before she could forbid him to go. The days were long and busy but, worst of all, full of terror, and this morning Simon intended to see for himself.

As Simon let himself out into the narrow street, he heard other sounds of life beginning to stir. The baker at the corner shop would have been up for hours, doling out the meagre ration of flour to bake bread. Housewives gathered their urns to collect water for cooking and washing, while the soldiers checked the battlements, dug ditches and strengthened the fortifications throughout the small town.

'Good morning.' Simon smiled at the baker as he passed. He hesitated; some mornings the baker slipped Simon an extra crust of bread, and he was so hungry all the time...the townspeople were beginning to starve. After seven long years the food had almost run out.

'Where are you off to?' The baker frowned, but he handed Simon a thick crust of yesterday's bread.

Simon didn't know whether to tell the truth – that was just asking for trouble – but before he could say anything the old man nodded. 'I suppose we're all in God's hands now,' he said, turning back to his oven.

Simon was thoughtful as he picked his way through the narrow streets. Since his family had taken refuge in the town seven years ago – almost as long as Simon could remember – people had hurried here and there, constantly busy, even though they knew every day might be their last one. But not this morning. The people on the streets moved slowly and smiled sadly to each other.

Three years ago, everything had changed when a new Roman general and his army had arrived and ordered the town to surrender. Until that time, the townspeople had thought they could hold out – they'd stored plenty of food and water, expecting a long siege; they'd even successfully fended off attacks. But since the new general, Simon hadn't set foot outside Masada. It was too dangerous. Not because of the high stone walls that surrounded the mountain fortress, nor the dangerous footpaths winding down to the valley, but because the Roman general and his army surrounded the entire mountain. Even the battlements weren't safe; the Romans fired arrows at any sentry foolish enough to leave his head up for too long.

Finally, Simon arrived at his destination. A lonely sentry looked down from the stone wall, and Simon ducked out of sight. But it was too late, the sentry had spotted him.

'You, boy! Go home. This is no place for children,' he shouted.

Simon stood his ground. He took a deep breath. 'I want to see,' he called. 'I want to see the Romans.'

For a moment the sentry eyed Simon, and then shrugged and smiled sadly. 'Why not? Come up, boy. But you can only stay for a moment.'

Simon climbed the stone steps to the short wooden ladder and looked out from the battlements. It was an impressive sight. Far below in the valley the Roman army was camped; in every direction hundreds and hundreds of tents were erected in straight military rows. There were fires, and the sound of hammering and swords and laughter drifted upwards.

Simon saw wooden structures rising high above the ground as the Romans constructed their catapults and siege machines. The valley was alive with colour and movement; mounted soldiers wheeled their horses and legionaries marched in tight formations. It was almost exciting, until Simon realised that even though Masada was built high on the side of a mountain, the Roman army besieging the town was big enough for the job.

'Take a good look.' The sentry pointed. 'See that wall there...'

Far below, a stone and earth wall encircled the *entire* valley. And along the top of the wall, Roman soldiers had built more wooden structures that were nearly as high as the town's walls.

'...it took them three years to build that wall,' the sentry continued. 'And tomorrow?' He shrugged and smiled at Simon. 'Who knows what will happen tomorrow. Now go home, boy. And pray.'

Simon took one last look before he scrambled

back down the ladder. So what his mother said was true: an entire Roman army had been sent to defeat this one tiny town. The Romans would never give up; even though they had lost battles, they would not lose the war.

It took all of Simon's courage to fight back tears. The people of the town said terrible things about the Romans: that all the people of Masada would be sold into slavery when the town was captured, if they were lucky. They were more likely to be punished as an example to other towns who might consider rebelling...they would be killed, or at least tortured. No one, not even the children, would be spared.

'Simon!' His mother called from the doorway. 'Where have you been? I've been looking for you everywhere.'

'Nowhere.' Simon would only get into more trouble if he confessed.

But his mother guessed correctly and shook her head. 'Oh, Simon. I told you not to talk to the soldiers. You're too young.'

'I'm not,' Simon retorted. 'I want to fight, too. I want to fight the Romans.'

Slowly, his mother sat down and began to cry.

'I understand, Simon,' she said between her tears. 'What happens tomorrow will happen to all of us. You're right. You are old enough. Go. Go and help the soldiers.'

She caught his sleeve before he could slip away. 'Have some breakfast first.' She offered him a crust of bread soaked in olive oil. A cup of watered wine. It was all they had.

Simon returned to the battlements. The noise grew louder as he approached. Hammering. Shouts. The sounds of swords. The smell of metal, of men and of fear. The Roman army was much closer.

'I've come to help,' Simon shouted up at the soldiers on the walls.

This time no one laughed and told him to go home. They set him to work tending the fires beneath a huge cauldron of black, sticky pitch. It had to be kept hot, very hot. Boiling, if possible, ready to pour over the Roman soldiers when they attacked the walls.

All day Simon carted wood for the fire, without complaint, and without anything to eat until his mother arrived with a small loaf of hard bread and a jug of water.

By nightfall, the Roman siege machines reached the height of Masada's walls. Simon could hear the enemy soldiers shouting orders to each other. They were close enough to smell. Simon closed his eyes and prayed.

A soldier tugged his sleeve.

'Come with me,' he whispered, pointing back inside the town.

Simon followed. All the soldiers, all the townspeople, were sneaking away from the outer wall, retreating behind the new barricades they'd built over the last year. The people of Masada waited, safe for the moment. They listened while the Romans smashed down the outer gates and set fire to the new barricades. Then the Romans

retreated to their camp to let the fire do its work. No doubt they would be back in the morning to finish off the job...

✳ ✳ ✳

The Romans did return in the morning. There was no resistance from the people of Masada. Every man, woman and child was dead. The people of Masada had killed themselves. Nearly one thousand people died.

A single woman and her children had escaped to hide in the mountains. When the Romans captured her, she told them what had happened. A contemporary Jewish historian, Josephus, reported that:

'An old woman escaped, along with another who was related to Eleazar, in intelligence and education superior to most women, and five little children. They had hidden in the conduits that brought drinking water underground while the rest were intent upon the suicide pact. These numbered nine hundred and sixty, women and children included.'

HISTORICAL MASADA

In the first century AD, the Jewish people living in and around Judea finally decided they were sick of Roman rule, and they revolted. Shortly afterwards, Roman armies arrived and wiped out the rebellion. A small group of Jewish people fled to a fortress town high on a mountain near the Dead Sea. That fortress was Masada. Soon enough, the Senate in Rome sent the Tenth Legion to deal with the last of the rebels. It took seven years, but on about 14 April AD 73, the army broke down the burned barricades and walked into the town. The Roman army had won the war, but at a terrible price for the people of Masada.

The story of Masada comes to us from several historical sources: letters and reports from the Romans themselves, other contemporary historians, and oral stories kept alive by the retelling. Are they accurate? Today, we're not sure. Recent archaeological evidence has clouded the picture – exactly who were the people in Masada and how did they die? It has been suggested that a small religious sect took refuge in Masada, and they may have been killed by their own soldiers.

Maybe we'll never know what really happened at Masada, but the stories will continue to be told and retold in the light of further investigation and new archaeological evidence.

ROMANS AT WAR

Walls surrounded many ancient cities and towns, built to protect them from attack. But even strong walls didn't stop the Roman armies. A lot of towns just surrendered as soon as a Roman army turned up, because they had a tough reputation. The Romans preferred to attack a town quickly, before the inhabitants were prepared, to get it all over and done with. But when they encountered a walled city like Masada that refused to surrender, they surrounded the walls and laid siege.

The object of a siege was to starve the people inside until they either surrendered or became weak enough to defeat. Rome took sieges very seriously. At the Siege of Rhodes in 305 BC, the Roman army built a siege tower so huge it took 3,500 soldiers to move it.

The ancient Romans were very good at building things. (So good that some ancient Roman roads are still useable in the twentieth century.) The first things the engineers built during a siege were huge earth walls around the town. Then they cut down trees from the closest forest and built wooden towers as high as the town's walls, making it easier for the soldiers to attack. Roman archers and artillery would stand on the towers and shoot arrows and hurl boulders directly into the town. Finally, the army would try to destroy the town's gates with huge battering rams.

Of course, the people inside the town defended themselves by setting fire to the wooden towers, and pouring boiling oil or water onto the soldiers. But the Roman army was persistent. It usually won. And if it didn't, another legion of Roman soldiers would turn up and keep trying until they did win.

Roman engineers also used timber to build some of the earliest artillery – machines designed to hurl things at the enemy. The Romans called these machines *tormenta*, but they had several drawbacks. They were difficult to aim, and because they were very heavy and hard to move, they were built where and when they were needed, and not transported with the army. So, for each battle, new siege towers and *tormenta* had to be built. But the army travelled faster because heavy war machines did not slow it down.

Tormenta were divided into two groups: *catapultae* were designed to shoot arrows and darts; *ballistae* were designed to hurl stones or huge beams of timber, and worked in principle like modern artillery or cannon. The largest *catapultae* were huge, and had to be mounted on strong wooden platforms.

War machines could also be used to hurl rotting dead animals, bits of people (especially their heads), or anything else nasty that came to hand. These missiles weren't particularly successful at destroying town walls, but they did terrify the people inside. Today, we would call this psychological warfare.

THE MIDDLE AGES

The Roman Empire finally collapsed when the Goths (very fierce nomadic tribes from central Europe) sacked the city of Rome. It was the end of an era. The glory of Rome was gone forever, and the empire broke up. The extensive Roman road network became impassable. Roman soldiers no longer marched from one corner of the empire to the other, and without the protection of Rome, trade and travel became too dangerous and almost ceased. Bridges and aqueducts fell into ruin. Communities became isolated. The remains of the Roman Empire relocated to Constantinople in Eastern Europe (modern Istanbul). In Western Europe, tribal chieftains fought over the land; the Vandals conquered north-west Africa, the Visigoths took Spain, and the Anglo-Saxons established strongholds in England.

There was virtually no central government. Life returned to a farming economy, and a system called feudalism developed. Serfs (or peasants) were at the very bottom of this system. They were not exactly slaves because they could not be bought and sold, but they were not free – they were economic slaves. Serfs could only leave their master's land with his permission. They had to pay him rent and work his land for several days a week without any wages. Anything the serfs did manage to grow or make for themselves was heavily taxed. And their master could force them into military service – to refuse

was to risk punishment and even death. For most people there was almost no travel, no education, no medicine.

But there was war. The local princes and kings fought each other continually, though both their arms and military tactics were primitive, generally involving brute force. They did throw things at each other, mainly during sieges, using slingshots and catapults developed by the Romans as war machinery many centuries earlier. But there were no explosives...yet.

Making Gunpowder

The ancient Chinese were the first people to discover that gunpowder could be created from a mixture of charcoal, sulphur and saltpetre. The details of their discovery have been lost in time. We don't know who first experimented with these primitive chemicals, but unless they got the technique exactly right the first time, there is a good chance the early Chinese chemists blew off their fingers (and other parts of their bodies) while they were perfecting the formula.

Why were they experimenting with gunpowder? Gunpowder was probably first used for fireworks, creating colourful and exciting explosions for the entertainment of the imperial Chinese court.

The chemicals in gunpowder provide the essential ingredients for combustion – heat, fuel and oxygen. Sulphur is an element that burns easily, charcoal provides fuel, and saltpetre releases oxygen when it burns. So all gunpowder requires is a source of ignition: a flame, or even a spark. Remember that gunpowder will only explode when it is confined in a small space, otherwise it burns with a single bright flash.

But let's consider those ancient Chinese chemists. Where did the chemicals come from? Charcoal is easy, you can find it in any fireplace, but sulphur in its pure form is usually found only around the edge of volcanoes. Volcanoes can lie quietly for decades, even hundreds of years, before finally exploding into life, and many ancient travellers risked their lives to bring back the strange yellow powder, sulphur.

Saltpetre was discovered by some shrewd observation. Saltpetre crystals form inside dung heaps soaked in animal or human urine. Maybe someone threw a handful of saltpetre crystals onto a fire and (if they weren't standing too close) was surprised when the flames flared up and burned brightly. It must have looked like magic.

FiReWoRKS

Today, in many places, fireworks are banned. (Hospitals got sick of treating burns and missing eyes and fingers.) Trained and licensed pyrotechnicians – explosives experts – control professional fireworks displays. And even they still make mistakes.

Traditional fireworks fall into several categories. Crackers are paper tubes (usually coloured red) packed with gunpowder and fired by lighting a fuse. They explode with a bang, and are designed to make noise. Crackers come in all shapes and sizes, from 'Tom Thumbs' only about a centimetre long to 'penny bungers' about the size of a finger. Catherine-wheels are designed to spin, with the fireworks set around the outside of a wheel. Roman candles are formed from long paper cylinders, and they spit out balls of fire or showers of sparks. Skyrockets are mounted on a stick, and are designed to explode high in the air – sometimes with colourful light displays. Colour is added to fireworks by mixing compounds of various metals which burn with different coloured flames. All of these fireworks can be assembled in combination with each other.

For the Year 2000 celebrations, tonnes of fireworks were exploded around the world in a single twenty-four hour period – from the spectacular golden showers of sparks from the Sydney Harbour Bridge, to the shooting stars on the Eiffel Tower in Paris. Just like the ancient Chinese, people still like to celebrate with fireworks.

ROMAN CANDLES AND CATHERINE-WHEELS

Roman candles took their name from a jolly little torture designed by the ancient Roman emperor Nero. The city of Rome was devastated by a fire that burned for over a week, and afterwards a small religious sect, called Christians, were blamed. Rumours at the time suggested Nero himself was responsible for the fire because he wanted to clear a large area in the centre of the city to expand his palace. But, whatever really happened, Nero ordered the Christians be put to death. They were bound in strips of cloth, covered in tar, tied to wooden poles and set alight as living torches. This was too ghastly for even the bloodthirsty Romans, and they were quick to spread nasty rumours about Nero.

Catherine-wheels were named after the torture and death of the Christian martyr St Catherine. She was condemned to death on the wheel (a ghastly torture involving breaking all the major bones in the body). But despite her torturers' best efforts, she continued to live. Finally, in frustration, they cut off her head.

GUNPOWDER AND WAR

Sooner or later, someone saw the potential for gunpowder in warfare. Ancient records suggest the earliest Chinese war rockets were in use by the seventh century, though they were probably used to frighten the enemy rather than cause destruction.

While people in Europe were still throwing things at each other, the Arabs were the first people to adopt gunpowder outside China. At first, the Arabs simply adopted the primitive Chinese war rockets and called them 'Chinese Arrows'. By the middle of the thirteenth century, the Arabs had developed a war rocket that could shoot arrows, but it was largely unsuccessful because the bamboo guns tended to blow apart.

Cannon were the first artillery to be developed. Their awesome firing power was demonstrated to the world during the capture of Constantinople.

THE FALL AND FALL OF CONSTANTINOPLE

Constantinople was one of the world's most besieged cities. It has a long and bloody history. Over the centuries just about everyone has tried to conquer Constantinople. In fact, armies have surrounded its ancient walls seven times.

It was Constantinople's good fortune, and also its bad luck, to be situated at the crossroads of Europe and Asia. It also had an excellent natural harbour, and all trade between east and west passed through Constantinople. So not only was Constantinople a city of wealth, education and culture, but it was also a rich prize for any ambitious emperor or king. Control Constantinople and you controlled the wealth of the trade routes.

Originally the city was an ancient trading town called Byzantium, but a Roman emperor in the fourth century AD decided to leave Rome and set up a new capital city. His name was Constantine, and even though he converted his empire to Christianity, it was not until he was dying that he himself became a Christian. He hadn't always been so charitable. Many years earlier (so the rumours went) Constantine arranged to have his wife locked in her bathroom with the heating turned up until she was cooked to death.

After Constantine's death, the city continued to flourish, and it became a major cultural centre where ancient manuscripts were copied and compiled into encyclopedias and reference books. Such a rich city had to be protected, and several emperors spent a lot of money doing just that, enclosing Constantinople behind impregnable walls – thirty-metre-high stone walls.

Of course, many greedy eyes examined Constantinople's walls with exactly the opposite idea – how to break inside and plunder the city's wealth.

Meanwhile, the new religion of Islam had swept through the Arab world, and, inspired, they turned their armies against the 'unbelievers' (or 'infidels'). Soon, Constantinople was the only Christian stronghold left standing in the Middle East. In the mid-seventh century, the Turkish armies arrived outside the city walls, and all seemed lost for the citizens of Constantinople, as a long siege of starvation began.

GReek FiRe

It would all have been over except for a man called
Callinicus. We don't know much about him except that he
came from Syria and threw in his lot with the Christian
emperor at Constantinople. Callinicus was an architect,
but he must also have been interested in chemistry. He
invented a substance called 'Greek fire'. Today, we don't
know exactly what Greek fire was – its formula has been
lost in time – but Callinicus discovered that a mixture
that included saltpetre, bitumen, sulphur and quicklime
produced a fire that could not be put out with water. We
do know that when water is added to quicklime (calcium
oxide), the chemical reaction produces immense heat, and
this was probably the basic secret of Greek fire.

The defenders of Constantinople rained Greek fire on
the Arabs and their warships in the harbour. When the
fire landed on the water it kept burning, and it set the
Arab ships alight, burning straight through the wooden
decks and sinking the ships. It also melted flesh. Men
writhed in agony as Greek fire burned through their
bodies. It was no use jumping into the water: once the fire
stuck to them they knew there was no hope of being
saved. It was an agonising death.

Constantinople was safe while they held the secret of
Greek fire. Over the centuries many armies tried to breach
Constantinople's famous walls. The Crusaders captured
the city for a while, but they were just passing through on
their way to the Holy Land. (The early Christian
community in Europe believed that the world would end
in the year 1000. When it didn't, they raised several 'holy'
armies over the next few centuries and attempted to

invade and 'liberate' the holy city of Jerusalem from Islam. The Christian Greeks followed suit).

The Turks made several attempts to capture Constantinople. Eventually the armies of the Ottoman Empire brought a new weapon with them – the siege cannon.

THe Siege cannon

The Turkish weapon-makers had been trying to make the biggest and most powerful cannons possible. The bronze siege cannons used at Constantinople were huge, about seven metres in length, with stone cannonballs weighing more than 300 kilograms. It took several people to lift a single cannonball. The massive siege cannons were also extremely difficult to move, but they didn't have to be brought close to the fighting action – the cannons could aim at targets from up to two kilometres away.

The new siege cannons demonstrated their might for the first time at Constantinople. It didn't take long. Once the walls were breached, Constantinople fell within hours, and on 29 May 1453 the Turks stormed the city. The emperor was killed and the Christian population was sold into slavery.

THE MONGOL TERROR

In the thirteenth century, Genghis Khan united the Mongol tribes. The Mongols were very fierce horse-riding warriors who came from the steppes of central Asia. It was (and still is) a hard land. Summer lasts barely three months of the year, and for the rest of the time fierce winds and snowstorms howl across the grassland plains. Perhaps not surprisingly, the Mongols and their horses were as tough as their land.

They were not only superb horsemen but also expert archers. The Mongol army was fast, light and agile. They fought on horseback and could travel over 200 kilometres a day. Soon they swept across Asia and Europe, conquering everything in their path.

Their leader, Genghis Khan, was undoubtedly a tactical genius.

There were many legends and stories about the Great Khan. Temujin was the son of a local tribal chieftain. When he was thirteen years old, his father was poisoned and died. Temujin's mother, brothers and sisters were banished by their tribe and left to fend for themselves. For several years they survived in this harsh land on their own. It made young Temujin tough and ruthless. His mother told him, 'Remember, you have no companions but your shadow.' One day his brother argued with him over a fish, and Temujin promptly killed him.

There were many more stories of Temujin's courage and ruthlessness, but it took him a few years of bloody war before he became the supreme ruler of the Mongol tribes. He took the name Genghis Khan, which means 'prince of all that lies between the oceans'.

The Mongol rules of war were simple: either you surrendered immediately and became their slaves, or you were massacred. When the Persians refused to surrender, Genghis Khan took his revenge. At a city called Bukhara, the Mongols set fire to all the wooden buildings and drove local hostages in front of their army as a living shield. Eventually Bukhara was taken, and Genghis ordered the 30,000 men who had defended the city to be slaughtered, and the women and children taken as slaves. The city was set alight and razed to the ground. It didn't pay to cross Genghis Khan.

After Genghis died, one of his sons continued the conquest of Eastern Europe, Russia and Poland. His army was poised to decimate the rest of Western Europe – but they stopped and went home instead.

THE TERROR CONTINUES

In the East and India, the brutality of the Mongols continued for more than a hundred years. Another of Genghis's sons, Toluy, carved out his career as a sadistic madman. At one city, Toluy ordered all the people to surrender and stand outside the city walls with their hands tied behind their backs. Tragically (and stupidly – they must have heard the Mongols' reputation by now) the people of the city did exactly what they were told. The Mongol army surrounded the people and rained wave after wave of arrows onto the helpless captives. They massacred everyone. If the people of Khorassan had tried to run and hide in the hills instead, many of them would probably have escaped.

Toluy got madder and his cruelty grew worse. When he was told people had escaped by hiding among the bodies and pretending to be dead, he ordered all the corpses' heads to be cut off and arranged in three pyramids – one for men, one for women, and one for children. Other Mongol warlords perfected this technique, erecting large towers built from severed heads. Not only were the Mongols celebrating their victory, but long after they left, the towers of heads would continue to terrify the local people – a gruesome reminder of the might of the Mongol empire.

But not all Mongols were this savage. One of Genghis's grandsons went on to conquer China and establish himself as emperor. Many years in the future, another young adventurer, Marco Polo, would meet Kublai Khan and bring back tales of China to Europe.

Surprisingly, the real heritage the Mongols gave Europe and Asia after the brutal invasions was a century of relative peace. For the first time since the Roman Empire, trade routes and travel between Europe and Asia were safe, and both goods (such as silk, spices, china and gold) and ideas (such as gunpowder) were exchanged. Merchants like Marco Polo began to make the journey, even though it was a long one: Marco Polo's travels to China and back took him twenty years.

Back to Europe

Let's not forget Europe was still in the grip of the Middle Ages and feudalism. The Church had become the centre of learning and education, so it wasn't surprising that the formula for gunpowder first appeared in the writing of a thirteenth-century Christian monk – Roger Bacon.

THE
ALCHEMISTS

THE ALCHEMIST'S APPRENTICE

Nicholas opened his eyes. His master stood above him, poking Nicholas with his foot.

'Up, boy, up! We have work to do.'

Nicholas groaned silently. What was his master up to now?

Although Nicholas was twelve years old, he didn't know the date of his birthday. Very few people could read or write, and nobody bothered to record the birth of a peasant's son.

Nicholas slept in a corner of his master's workroom, and for a moment he pulled his head back under the stiff woollen blanket. Both the thin straw mattress and the blanket were itchy, not the least for the fleas and lice that lived there. But he was lucky his head was shaven and he was too young for a beard, otherwise the lice would be worse.

Briefly, Nicholas scratched at the scabs on his body and legs before he pulled his robe over his head. It was also made of itchy wool, but as it was Nicholas's only garment, he was glad of its warmth. With a cord he fastened the robe around his body, and slipped rough leather sandals on his feet. Nicholas was proud of his sandals, even though the monks taught him pride was a sin. Before he came to live at the monastery he wore only bare feet, even in the deepest winter snows.

But that was the least of his problems at the moment.

'Yes, master?' Nicholas presented himself. It was still early. Outside Nicholas could hear the bells summoning the monks to first prayers before daylight. Whatever his master wanted must be urgent.

It was Nicholas's job to keep the workroom clean and attend to any simple errands. The shelves and wooden tables were covered with stone jars and precious glass bottles. Nicholas had learned to be cautious. Many of the jars contained substances that not only smelled bad, but were also dangerous. On the shelves were a few ancient scrolls and hand-copied books. Although Nicholas couldn't read, he knew the books were extremely precious. Irreplaceable. If the books were damaged Nicholas would be beaten, punished, perhaps even thrown out of the monastery.

This morning his master was working with a mortar and pestle filled with black powder. Nicholas waited nervously until his master paused and looked up from his workbench.

'Ah, Nicholas!' he said. 'Bring the candle closer.'

Nicholas edged forward. The grainy black powder looked innocent enough, and Nicholas knew that at least some of the mysterious mixture was just crushed charcoal from the fireplace. But there were other substances as well: a foul-smelling yellow powder, and small crystals his master collected from the dungheaps near the monastery walls.

'Let's try it, shall we?' Nicholas's master took the candle and motioned Nicholas to stand back. Nicholas swallowed nervously, watching as his master tipped the black powder onto the stone bench and carefully brought the candle flame closer.

Poof!

A bright flash of light as the black powder burst into flames! And a strange, unpleasant smell. Nicholas crossed himself. It was the devil's work, surely.

His master looked very pleased, but eventually he noticed Nicholas's pale cheeks and shaking knees.

'Have you had breakfast?' his master asked.

Nicholas shook his head.

'Be quick about it. We have much work to do.'

The young apprentice took a tallow candle, happy to leave the workroom. The candle smoked, covering Nicholas with filthy black soot, but he didn't know he was filthy. He had never had a bath in his life because people believed washing was unhealthy and could lead to sickness.

It was gruel again for breakfast. It was the same every morning – a thin porridge made from boiled grains, but it was hot. And there was sour beer to drink, a bitter brew diluted with water. At lunch, if Nicholas was lucky, there might be a slice of hard black bread. It was tough to chew, but Nicholas's teeth were still strong. The older monks had to soak their crusts in beer before they could chew them. Occasionally there were boiled green vegetables and once or twice on feast days perhaps an egg or a piece of boiled meat.

Nicholas was still hungry when he finished, but he had learnt to be grateful. Many more people outside the monastery starved to death in the hard winters. And the winters had been particularly hard these last few years.

Quickly, Nicholas finished eating and returned to the workshop. The door was ajar and he could hear voices. Did his master have a visitor, or was he talking to himself again? Lately, his master had been behaving quite strangely, and Nicholas was frightened. Once he overheard the other monks whispering – something about a book his master wrote for the Pope. Everyone at the monastery was waiting to hear what the Pope would say about the book. They were worried.

'Nicholas!' his master called.

Nicholas took a deep breath and pushed open the door. Oh, no! His master's visitor was the Abbot. The Abbot rarely came to the monastery, and by the look on his face something dreadful was going to happen.

'Collect my things, Nicholas. I may be away for a while,' his master said.

'Douse the fire and put out the candles.' The Abbot smiled grimly. 'Your master is charged with heresy.'

Nicholas froze in terror. Heresy! A crime against the Church. What would happen to his master? What would happen to him? Nicholas knew the stories, of the rack, of terrible torture. Not for the first time Nicholas was truly afraid.

Much later, Nicholas heard that his master was imprisoned. The apprentice was a grown man before Roger Bacon was released.

240 million
First dinosaurs

THE MASTER ALCHEMIST

Why was Roger Bacon experimenting with gunpowder? Almost certainly he had read about the 'black powder' in manuscripts brought back from Arabia after the Mongol invasion.

Roger Bacon was one of the most important thinkers of his time. In Europe in the mid-thirteenth century, ancient books were being rediscovered after being lost for centuries. Roger Bacon came from a wealthy family and was well educated, studying at the very first universities in Oxford and Paris. He became a monk and continued his studies in alchemy, optics and astronomy. But he held revolutionary ideas, ideas that would land him in prison.

Roger Bacon believed that instead of relying on ancient books, learning should be based on experiments and observations. According to the Church, this was heresy and Roger Bacon was a heretic (and perhaps even a witch). Heresy was a crime punishable by death.

The word heretic is taken from a Greek word meaning 'to choose for oneself'. Heresy simply meant you didn't agree with what the Church told you to believe. Now, the Church in the Middle Ages viewed independent thinking and experimentation as extremely dangerous – possibly the work of the devil. Poor Roger Bacon spent ten years in prison and his books were banned. Happily for him, the Church authorities eventually let him out and he was free to continue his studies.

Most importantly, Roger Bacon's heresy paved the way for the development of modern science using observation and experiment.

THE PHILOSOPHER'S STONE

Although medieval alchemists were experimenting with gunpowder, it was not what they were looking for – they were searching for the Philosopher's Stone.

In the light of present-day science, the search for the Philosopher's Stone sounds bizarre. In fact the alchemists weren't looking for a stone, but a magical substance which could transform metal into gold. This, of course, would make them instantly rich and powerful. They also believed this magical substance would grant them eternal youth; it would be the Elixir of Life and they could enjoy all that gold and power for a very long time.

In many ways alchemy was the forerunner of chemistry, and even though it was often by accident, the alchemists discovered many new substances. With the advent of scientific experiment, the bangs were about to get bigger.

FULMinatinG GOLD

The alchemists continued to experiment, but not all of their discoveries were practical.

Fulminating gold was used briefly as an explosive in the European wars of the early seventeenth century. First the alchemists dissolved a lot of gold in a mixture of concentrated acids, and after further processing they ended up with a new explosive. But fulminating gold was too expensive to make in large quantities. No city could afford to defend itself using fulminating gold. It would be centuries until a cheaper, more effective explosive than gunpowder was discovered.

Mastering the Art of Bigger Bangs

All explosives work when chemical compounds burn rapidly (or in the case of atomic explosions, decompose rapidly), generating large amounts of gas and heat.

Remember gunpowder will only explode if it's confined, otherwise the air can absorb the gas and heat, and it simply burns with a bright flame. Gunpowder was probably man's most dangerous invention until the atomic bomb. It changed the rules of warfare forever.

Explosive Propellants

Initially, gunpowder was used as an explosive propellant. It was not the gunpowder that caused injury and destruction, but the hurtling cannonballs. The explosive energy of gunpowder had to be harnessed.

There's a trick to using explosive propellants. If the explosion creates a sudden shock, the gun or cannon is likely to blow up, which was fatally bad news for the person standing next to it. A cannon was no use if it exploded and killed off your own men.

EARLY GUNS

To be effective, the explosive propellant must burn slowly, and the explosion must deliver a steadily increasing force to the projectile in the barrel of the gun. To achieve this, not only did gunpowder manufacture have to improve, but also the smelting and casting of metal.

We don't know exactly who discovered gunmetal (or when). Gunmetal is a high copper alloy that also contains tin and zinc. An alloy is simply a metal blended with other substances. Gunmetal was used to cast cannons because it was tough, hard-wearing and resisted corrosion – it didn't rust. And it wasn't as likely to blow up in your face.

LAWS, GUNS AND MONEY

Laws controlling the manufacture of gunpowder were introduced in England during the seventeenth century. There were probably two good reasons for this. Gunpowder needed to be reliable – otherwise expensive weapons could be destroyed, and in the middle of a battle that could be disastrous. And there was money to be made out of gunpowder.

During the reign of Queen Elizabeth I, the manufacture of gunpowder in England became a monopoly of the Crown. That is, only the royal explosives experts were allowed to make and sell gunpowder. It is interesting to note that when Queen Elizabeth I came to the throne, England was in financial trouble, but when she died there was lots of gold in the treasury. Of course, the monopoly was not the only reason – by then the English navy was sailing around the known world, bringing trade and new wealth back to England.

MUZZLE-LOADING GUNS

While the Turkish armies were using massive siege cannon successfully against Constantinople, back in Western Europe the weapon-makers were interested in something different: they were learning how to cast artillery that was more mobile and faster to fire. Eventually, they would invent a cannon that was so small and light it could be carried and operated by one person – they invented the gun.

There were two major practical problems to be overcome before guns could be safely used. How to load the gunpowder into the gun, and how to ignite the gunpowder without injury.

The first small arms were basically miniature cannon. At this stage, guns were metal tubes that were open at one end. Gunpowder was carefully poured through the opening into the tube, and then packed down tightly using a long, straight length of metal – a ramrod. Then the shot was poured in and the procedure repeated.

There was still one big problem to overcome – how to ignite the gunpowder inside the tube. It was extremely dangerous to set fire to the gunpowder from the front, down the barrel. A soldier risked blowing off his hands and/or his head. So the weapon-makers tried drilling a small 'touch-hole' at the closed end of the barrel. The soldier had to poke a red-hot wire into the tiny hole to ignite the gunpowder. This must have been easier said than done. It was a tricky manoeuvre, and took a steady hand and a cool mind in the middle of a battle.

KEEP YOUR GUNPOWDER DRY

The poor soldier had more problems. If his gunpowder was wet, or even damp, it would not explode, rendering his weapon useless. So these early guns were unreliable in wet or very humid weather. And the metal tubes were difficult to hold and aim. For once, this was a relatively simple problem: by attaching a piece of shaped wood to one end (not the open end!), the weapon-makers created a stock that could fit under one arm.

But igniting the gunpowder remained a problem. Someone came up with the idea of making a shallow depression around the outside of the touch-hole. Just

before the soldier wanted to fire his gun, he poured a small charge of dry gunpowder into the depression and set it alight from the outside. The small explosion in the 'flashpan' (named after the small 'flash' of burning gunpowder) ignited the gunpowder packed in the barrel of the gun, which exploded and fired out the shot. Even though the gunpowder could still get wet in the flashpan, it was an important step forward and much easier than poking a red-hot wire through a small hole. These early guns were called Firelocks. Other developments included the Matchlock gun, where a slow-burning fuse ignited the gunpowder in the flashpan; and the Flintlock, which used the spark from a flint to ignite the gunpowder.

But guns still had to be loaded down the barrel, so the soldier had to lower his rifle while he reloaded. This all took time, time when the soldier was vulnerable to attack. And it still took two hands to fire a gun. It would take another hundred years to develop percussion ignition and the modern bullet.

BReecH anD BULLeTs

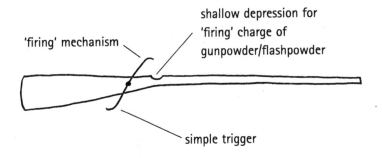

'firing' mechanism

shallow depression for 'firing' charge of gunpowder/flashpowder

simple trigger

A Scottish clergyman, the Reverend Alexander James Forsyth, invented percussion ignition. He discovered a way to make gunpowder explode by impact. He replaced the gunpowder in the touch hole with 'detonating powder' (composed mainly of potassium chlorate) which could be ignited by the force of a striking mechanism, which in turn ignited the gunpowder in the barrel of the gun. The invention of the percussion cap in 1807 and the subsequent invention of the self-contained cartridge would make it possible to load guns through the rear of the barrel – breech-loading firearms – which eventually led to the development of cartridges and bullets. At last the soldier could reload his rifle quickly!

Modern bullets have percussion caps built into their shell casing so just striking can detonate them. Bullets, even without a gun, are extremely dangerous. Hit them and they can explode in your face.

Of course, since then guns have developed in leaps and bounds. They can be fired automatically, aimed by laser beam, fitted with silencers. But effectively they all do the same thing. Kill things.

65 million Asteroid wipes out dinosaurs

Guns are only as stupid as the people holding them. People die in stupid gun deaths every year.

In December 1992, Ken Barger of North Carolina, USA, was asleep in bed. Unfortunately, Ken had the habit of keeping a loaded hand gun beside his bed in case of burglars. But the phone rang in the middle of the night, and Ken grabbed the gun by mistake. He held it up to his ear and shot himself dead.

In 1982, David Grundman was playing around with a shotgun in the desert in Arizona. David was shooting at a cactus. A very tall cactus. David shot the cactus, it fell over and crushed him to death.

Even armed robbers manage to shoot themselves. In 1975, a very nervous young man tried to hold up a restaurant in Newport, Rhode Island. He demanded money and put it in a small bag. Unfortunately, the would-be robber tried to stuff the bag into his shirt pocket while he was still holding the gun. The gun went off under his chin. He was killed instantly. The people in the restaurant were stunned.

In Seattle in 1996, a pair of bumbling robbers tried to hold up a grocery store. They both pulled out guns and threatened the store clerk. But one robber accidentally fired his gun, shooting his companion, who squeezed the trigger of his gun. The robbers shot each other, and, bleeding, they limped away from the store. The police followed the trail of blood to a hospital and arrested them both.

KILLING THINGS ON A BIGGER SCALE

All guns and cannon work by using an explosive charge to send a projectile (a bullet or a cannonball) slamming into a wall or a person. It is the projectile that does the damage. Bombs are more effective at large-scale death and destruction than hand guns and artillery.

Bombs are primarily designed to cause damage and death by the force of the blast and heat. They can be made more effective by adding shrapnel (nasty things such as bits of metal or nails) to improve their destructive power. But until the development of a better delivery system, bombs had limited use in warfare: the person lighting the bomb almost certainly risked being blown up by the explosion. For really effective bombs, you need something more powerful than gunpowder.

A new explosive chemical compound was discovered in 1846 – nitroglycerine. Unfortunately, nitroglycerine proved to be extremely dangerous to use. It was very poisonous and, more significantly, very unstable. Nitroglycerine was so sensitive it could explode with the smallest shock. Before the development of modern techniques, it was almost impossible to transport safely. But it remained an attractive explosive because it is at least eight times more powerful than gunpowder.

A man called Alfred Nobel taught the world how to use nitroglycerine safely.

ALFReD NOBel

Alfred Nobel was born to a wealthy family in Stockholm in Sweden in 1833. His father owned explosives factories in St Petersburg, so young Alfred was sent to university there, and later in the USA. By all accounts, Alfred Nobel was a well-educated and cultured man – he spoke several languages, travelled widely and wrote poetry.

After completing his studies, he returned to work in the family business – making mines, torpedoes and other explosives. Tragedy struck the Nobel family when Alfred's younger brother and four other people were killed in a factory accident. Nitroglycerine was still proving deadly to handle. Inspired by his brother's death, Alfred turned his talents to developing a safe way to handle nitroglycerine, and in 1867 he used a packing material to make the nitroglycerine more stable. He called this new substance dynamite. Later, he went on to invent ballistite – one of the first smokeless explosive powders. The family business was a raging success.

NOBEL PRIZE

Alfred Nobel became very wealthy. Seriously rich.

When Alfred died, he controlled explosives factories all over the world. But in his will, he left most of his money to fund prizes that would be awarded every year. The prizes were to be for outstanding work in physics, chemistry, medicine, literature and world peace. These became known as the Nobel Prizes, and they are still awarded every year. The Nobel Prizes are among the most prestigious in the world.

A Nobel Prize winner is known as a laureate. In ancient Greece a laurel wreath was awarded to the winner of the Olympic games – it was a symbol of supreme distinction, of being the very best.

A MODERN WAY WITH EXPLOSIVES

EARLY BOMBS

WHEN YOU GET CLOSE TO THE GROUND LIGHT THE FUSE OK?

TNT was developed not long after dynamite. Trinitrotoluene (TNT) can be handled, stored and used with even greater safety than dynamite, and by World War I it became the explosive of choice.

Almost as soon as the first aircraft was invented, someone thought about its potential for warfare. Just before World War I, the first Italian aviators threw explosive devices from their aircraft onto the Arab forces in Libya. At last the bomb-makers had a safe method of delivery. Since then the delivery of bombs has continued to progress. Surface-to-Air-Missiles. Smart Bombs. Laser Guidance. Modern technology has allowed us to deliver bombs with almost pinpoint accuracy.

Mines Continue To Kill

TNT is also the favourite explosive used in mines. There are two basic types of mines – landmines and water mines. They are weapons of war designed to destroy or disable enemy troops, ships and vehicles. But mines aren't smart, they also blow up innocent people and animals.

Mines are buried in the ground, or dropped in the ocean – then you leave. Sooner or later someone will set them off. They can be triggered by pressure (that is, you step on it) or by trip-wires (you disturb the wire), or by delayed action (set to explode at a certain time). Water mines can also be magnetic, designed to detonate when they detect the magnetic field of the metal hull of passing ships. Mines are also laid to make land routes (or waterways such as harbours and shipping lanes) too dangerous to use.

Unfortunately, even after the war is over, the mines are still there, silent and patient killers. For decades afterwards, innocent people will have their legs blown off – farmers trying to work the land to feed their families, children playing in the fields. Thousands and thousands of people are killed and maimed by landmines long after the fighting is over.

There are still millions of active mines all over the world, just waiting...

COULD BANGS GET ANY BIGGER?

Of course, explosives can be used for useful and peaceful purposes: quarrying, demolition, setting rivets (in industry), forming metals – even fireworks. But their greatest potential still remains with death and destruction.

During World War II, the scientists really got moving on this project, and by the end of the war they had created a bomb that contained a handful of explosives about the size of a baseball. It was the equivalent of 20,000 tonnes of TNT. Once again, the rules of warfare were about to change forever.

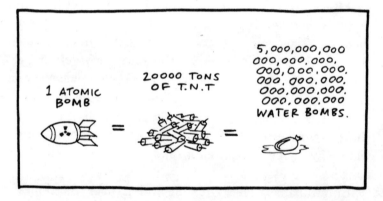

BANG-
YOU'RE
DEAD

A 'NUCLEAR TAN'

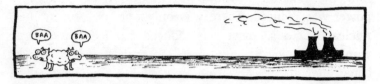

It was a warm spring morning when Olaf unlocked the wire fence enclosing the monitoring station. Olaf was studying at university, and part of his duties involved checking the observation equipment every morning. Mostly, it was boring routine work, but this morning his eyes nearly popped out of his head. He tapped the little dials and looked again. He checked the paper printout, shaking his head in disbelief. Could the equipment be faulty?

Olaf decided to call his supervisor out of bed, and a little while later both men scratched their heads. Olaf's supervisor made a phone call – radiation levels were twenty per cent above normal. It was serious. Both men looked eastwards towards the Soviet Union and the prevailing winds. Something had happened, something terrible.

The world held its breath. The Soviet government was silent.

Only a few days previously, people in the northern Ukraine were looking forward to the weekend. It was Friday, they made plans for picnics and family gatherings. Some of them planned to take advantage of the warm spring weather and do some sunbathing. What they didn't know was that the local nuclear plant was preparing to run efficiency tests at Reactor Four.

The night shift at Reactor Four started the tests at 1.00 a.m. on Saturday morning. The tests involved seeing how long the generators would run if the nuclear reactor's power was reduced. There was only one problem. If the nuclear reactor's power was reduced, the safety systems would shut everything down. Unfortunately, someone came up with the idea that they should shut down the safety systems to prevent this from happening. For a moment everything seemed fine.

Then the explosions began.

For the next twenty-three minutes, explosion after explosion destroyed the control systems in Reactor Four. Shocked, the staff of the nuclear plant were slow to react. Valery Pererozchenko, the plant foreman, desperately tried to get back to the control room, but what he saw on his journey made his blood run cold. The lids on the reactor cores were dancing in the air – he knew each lid weighed over 350 kilograms. Something dreadful was about to happen.

It didn't take long. Fifty-eight seconds later, two massive explosions blew the Reactor Four building apart. Thousands of tonnes of radioactive materials were spewed high into the atmosphere, and the smell of ozone filled the air.

A deadly plume of radioactivity soared over eleven kilometres into the sky before spreading out over the countryside. Fanned by the winds, the radioactive cloud slowly drifted towards Olaf's monitoring station in Sweden.

It was chaos inside the reactor plant. Temperatures soared to over 2500°C, flames leapt thirty metres into the air. It was impossible to put out the fires with water.

Desperately the firefighters threw sand onto the flames, trying to ignore the melting, burning radioactive asphalt sticking to their boots. It was almost useless.

People began to die. Almost immediately two plant workers died quick and horrible deaths from the intense radiation.

But someone was still thinking. The deputy chief of the electrical section, Aleksander Lelechenko, plunged back inside the building. Even though he knew the radioactivity would kill him, he made a heroic attempt to restart the reactor cooling system. He waded through radioactive water, past piles of highly radioactive debris. But it was too late. The cooling system was already destroyed. There was nothing he could do. He made his way back outside, and although Lelechenko received first aid, he died not long after.

In the towns nearby, the people were unaware of the accident at the nuclear plant. A man was sunbathing in his backyard when he noticed he'd acquired a tan after only a few minutes. He went inside to show his friends, just before he started vomiting and fell to the floor, twitching with convulsions. Within the hour he was dead, still unaware of the cause of his 'nuclear tan'.

Eventually the Soviet government reacted. They issued a short statement to the world. There had been an accident at the Chernobyl nuclear plant, but everything was under control. They refused all offers of help.

Everything was not under control. It was not until thirty-six hours after the initial accident that the evacuations began, and the specialised firefighters arrived. By then, thousands of people had been exposed to enough radiation to kill them.

CHERNOBYL

The death count at Chernobyl in 1995 was at least 125,000. People are still dying. Towns and farms within a thirty-kilometre radius were evacuated, and they became ghost towns. Everything had to be abandoned: farm animals, livestock, houses, furniture, tools, toys, and even clothes. It was all contaminated by radioactivity.

It is estimated that eventually four million people will die as a result of the nuclear accident at Chernobyl. In surrounding areas, birth defects have increased at an alarming rate. Horses are born with eight deformed legs, pigs with no eyes. Radiation does not stop at national borders. As far away as Italy, meat was found to be contaminated by radioactivity.

At Chernobyl, helicopters eventually dumped huge quantities of concrete onto Reactor Four, encasing it in a permanent sarcophagus. Even so, the radiation levels will be deadly for hundreds of years to come.

Sadly, although Chernobyl was the most serious nuclear accident, there have been others – in the USA and England. But the story of nuclear energy has always been accompanied by tragedy.

500,000
First homo
sapiens

MaD scientists?

It all began innocently enough. Around the turn of the century, scientists were studying new and exciting developments: the discovery of photography and how to record actual images with light sensitive chemicals; the mystery of X-rays, which penetrated the body and revealed the structure of the skeleton.

In 1898, a French scientist, Marie Curie, discovered radium and investigated its radioactive effects.

In 1905, Albert Einstein published his theory that mass and energy are one – matter, because of its mass, is equivalent to an amount of energy fixed by Einstein's famous equation:

$E = mc^2$

This is a simple equation for a big idea. E stands for energy, m for mass, and c for the speed of light. The speed of light is a very big number – 300,000 kilometres per second. So, even a tiny mass when multiplied by the square of the speed of light (an enormous number) must contain truly enormous amounts of potential energy. Of course, the hard part is safely using and harnessing this energy.

Ernest Rutherford, a New Zealand scientist working in England, described how an atom was structured in 1911. He discovered that, rather than being a tiny piece of matter, atoms are mostly made up of space. The mass of an atom is concentrated in its centre (the nucleus), and it is orbited by minute satellites he named electrons. Electrons carry a negative electrical charge, while the nucleus is positive. Some atoms have a few electrons that are only loosely attached. These 'free electrons' can jump from atom to atom, and with them carry electrical charge.

All three discoveries were essential to the development of nuclear energy. The potential came closer to reality.

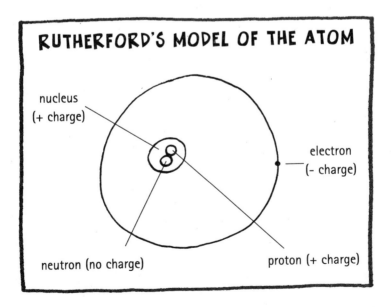

RUTHERFORD'S MODEL OF THE ATOM

nucleus
(+ charge)

electron
(- charge)

neutron (no charge)   proton (+ charge)

DEATH BY RESEARCH

Madame Marie Curie was born in Warsaw (Poland) in 1867. Her father was a schoolteacher, teaching high-school physics. She was destined to follow in his footsteps, and she studied physics at the famous Sorbonne University in Paris. Marie was a brilliant student, taking first place in the year she received her degree for physics. Not long after she graduated she met Pierre Curie (another physicist) and they married.

Marie became a research scientist. She was very interested in the recently discovered invisible radiation of X-rays, and uranium. Marie identified a new element – radium. She was the first person to use the term radioactive to describe the emission of invisible particles (which we now know is caused by the spontaneous disintegration of atomic nuclei).

Later the Curies worked together discovering another two elements. They were true scientific pioneers. Some of their laboratories were no more than wooden sheds, filled with equipment they'd begged and borrowed. But in 1903 the Curies received the Nobel Prize in Physics. Finally, they were given a special laboratory and money arrived from all over the world. In America, women raised $50,000 to help fund Marie's research. The Curies had two daughters, one of whom followed in her parents' footsteps: Irene Curie earned the Nobel Prize in Chemistry in 1935.

Tragically, a few years after Pierre and Marie won the Nobel Prize, Pierre was killed in a street accident when he was run over by a horse-drawn cart. Despite her grief,

Marie continued their research, and in 1911 she received a second Nobel Prize for Chemistry.

Marie Curie did not have to fight for funding again, but tragedy continued to haunt the Curie family. At the time Marie was experimenting, nobody knew about the dangers of radioactivity, and her long years of exposure to radioactivity finally killed her. She developed leukemia and died in 1934. Irene would die from the same cause.

THE BRAIN OF A GENIUS

Albert Einstein was born in Germany in 1879. As a young child he was not obviously a genius. Albert was nearly three years old before he began to talk, and his school record was not much better: he failed subjects and was asked to leave school. He repeated a year and re-sat the exams. His final university marks were so dismal he could not get a job. Eventually a relative helped find him employment as an office clerk.

But Albert Einstein did not waste his time. Armed with a pencil, paper and a brain, he continued to think and work. At the age of twenty-six, he published his Special Theory of Relativity. Ten years later he published his General Theory of Relativity, which turned the scientific world on its head. Many scientists could not understand what Einstein was talking about – his ideas were so radical, a violent debate raged for years in the scientific community. He won the 1924 Nobel Prize in Physics. Finally, he was acclaimed a genius.

But the political climate in Germany was changing. The Nazis came to power and their leader, Adolf Hitler, turned his hatred towards Albert Einstein. Einstein's property was confiscated, and he left Germany for the USA, which welcomed him with open arms.

Einstein died in America in 1955. After his death his brain was removed and preserved for scientific study. Pieces of Einstein's brain still sit in laboratory jars today.

Meet Me in Manhattan

Scientists began to wonder if Einstein's theory of the enormous power locked inside atomic structure could be harnessed to produce energy. Other scientists continued this work, but World War II interrupted them. Many scientists fled to America and England trying to escape the Nazis in Europe. The world held its breath while the war raged.

Albert Einstein wrote a letter to the American President during World War II suggesting an atomic weapon could be developed. President Franklin Roosevelt was interested, and although Albert Einstein wasn't directly involved, a group of scientists from all over the world came together for the Manhattan Project. In the New Mexico desert the scientists set to work. As they began to realise the destructive potential of the atom bomb, many of them began to have doubts and dropped out of the project.

But in the end it wasn't up to the scientists.

Although Germany surrendered in May 1945, the Japanese army was still fighting. It was decided that the atomic bomb would be dropped on two Japanese cities, Hiroshima and Nagasaki.

HiRoSHiMa

A bridge in the centre of Hiroshima was the
first target – the Aloi bridge. On a warm
summer morning, a single bomber
aircraft flew high above Hiroshima. In the streets below it
was morning. Briefly, an air
raid sounded, but as it was
only a single plane, the all
clear was quickly given
and everyone went back to
what they were doing.

Many children had been
evacuated to the countryside,
but older children formed
squads to help with demolition
work – clearing the debris from
previous bombing raids. Families were
having breakfast. Men and women
were on their way to work. It was
8:15 a.m.

There was a blinding flash of
brilliant light above Hiroshima.
The atomic bomb missed the
Aloi bridge by about 300
metres. It exploded in the air
directly above the Shima Surgical
Hospital. The bridge remained
standing even though it was damaged.
The hospital building and its patients and
staff were instantly vaporised.

The atomic bomb exploded with the force of about 15,000 tonnes of TNT. The air around the point of impact (or hypocentre) was heated to 300,000°C – thirty times hotter than the surface of the sun. Intense heat, radiation and a blast wave exploded across Hiroshima.

High above the city, a huge mushroom-shaped cloud formed in the sky. Below, the city burst into fire, and the first shock wave blasted the streets into piles of rubble. Close to the hypocentre granite buildings exploded, steel and stone melted. Further out wooden houses burst into flames, and broken windows blasted shattered glass across the streets. Fires raged across the entire city. Intense firestorms and whirlwinds engulfed Hiroshima. Every clock and watch stopped at exactly the same time – 8:15 – silenced forever by the blast of the shock wave.

Within an hour, 70,000 residents of Hiroshima were dead. Men, women and children wandered naked in the streets, their clothes either burnt or blown off, their skin terribly charred.

People did not recognise each other: some lost their faces, others had the shadow of their noses burnt into their cheeks. The people of Hiroshima thought they were in hell. Perhaps they were.

A little while later, condensation in the explosive cloud fell as 'black rain'. It not only contained radioactive soot and dust, it was also oily, sticking to everything it fell on – buildings, clothing and people. The black rain spread radioactive contamination even in areas a long way from the hypocentre. Another 130,000 Japanese would lose their lives from dreadful burns and radiation sickness.

Three days later a second atomic bomb was dropped on Nagasaki. Japan surrendered.

HOW DOES an ATOMIC BOMB WORK?

If two pieces of radioactive material are slammed together with great force (using an explosive charge), within a microsecond a chain reaction is triggered.

Again and again, atomic particles slam into each other, releasing huge amounts of energy. This is *nuclear fission* (splitting atoms). Uranium is a fission fuel, and although there is plenty of uranium on Earth, the active ingredient (Uranium 235) is quite rare.

I'VE MADE THIS ATOMIC BOMB OUT OF AN OLD MICROWAVE OVEN AND MY GLOW-IN-THE-DARK WATCH

YOU'RE BLUFFING

3000 BC
Earliest cities

The almost instantaneous release of energy heats the surrounding air (and anything else) to super-hot temperatures. The air explodes, forming a shock wave that follows a few moments later. The blast wave and radiation cause most of the death and destruction.

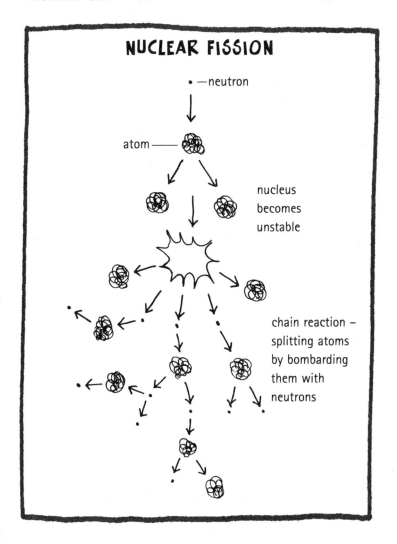

NUCLEAR FISSION

• —neutron

atom —

nucleus becomes unstable

chain reaction – splitting atoms by bombarding them with neutrons

Nuclear Fusion

It needs to be hot, very hot, to start *nuclear fusion* (fusing atoms). About 100 million degrees Celsius is needed to fuse hydrogen atoms together to create new atoms of helium. Stars, including our sun, are fuelled by nuclear fusion. Nuclear fusion can also be harnessed to create atomic weapons: the hydrogen bomb uses the more common forms of hydrogen as fuel, which, unlike uranium, are readily available and cheap. A hydrogen bomb needs a small nuclear fission bomb to create the high temperatures required to start the process.

The sun is like a huge hydrogen bomb – releasing its energy as heat and light. Fortunately for us, the sun's massive gravity prevents the nuclear reaction from going out of control.

Nuclear Winter

Immediately after World War II, people all over the world began to protest about the use of nuclear weapons. One of the first protest movements was 'Ban the Bomb' – there have been many since. But it was not until 1983 that a group of scientists came together and put forward the most frightening argument against the use of nuclear weapons. They believed that, even though there were enough weapons to destroy most life on earth, what might happen afterwards would be even more terrible.

After the initial explosions from an all-out nuclear war, the atmosphere would fill with dust, smoke, soot and ash. Within a short time, the cloud of ash and smoke would circle the earth, blotting out all the sun's rays.

Quickly, the earth would grow cold, plant life and animals would die. Snow and icy winds would blow across the earth, and when finally the ash and dust settled, the sun's rays would be reflected back into space. It would be a long time before the earth was warm enough to support animal life again.

War of the Worlds

After World War II ended, the Manhattan project was closed down and the scientists returned to other projects. Some of them began to daydream about the writings of an English writer. Long before Hiroshima, H.G.Wells wrote about a future where science would change people's lives forever. He was one of the first science-fiction writers.

Herbert George Wells was a young man when his first novel, *The Time Machine*, was published in 1895. A few years later he published *The War of the Worlds*, a story about Martian spaceships attacking Earth. He wrote about travelling through space to the moon, and this was several years before the first aircraft was invented! Many of H.G.Wells's predictions came to pass. He inspired a generation of young scientists and, in 1969, they realised one of his dreams when the first man walked on the moon.

THE NIGHT ALIENS INVADED AMERICA

In 1938, a young American actor produced a radio play based on H.G.Wells's novel *The War of the Worlds*. Orson Welles had founded the Mercury Theatre a year earlier, and already the company was known for producing unusual stage and radio dramas. (This was before TV was widely available and everyone listened to the radio in the evenings.) *The War of the Worlds* created a sensation. For the first time, a radio play was broadcast as though it was a real event, actually happening while people were listening.

On 30 October, the music on the radio was interrupted by an urgent news bulletin – a strange object was reported to have fallen from the sky near a little town in New Jersey. Scientists were on their way to investigate. The radio audience could hear sirens and crowds in the background. It sounded very serious.

The music resumed only to be interrupted by a further report that the object had landed. It was a mysterious metal cylinder, and there was a reporter on the scene...

'Ladies and gentlemen, this is the most terrifying thing I have ever witnessed...Wait a minute! Someone's crawling out of the hollow top. Someone or...something. I can see peering out of that black hole two luminous discs...are they eyes? It might be...'

Horrified, the reporter continued to describe tentacles; saliva dripping from its quivering, pulsating mouth; how the police arrived and approached the spaceship, only to be cut down in flames by the alien's death ray.

The station cut to an urgent new report from New York, where a reporter described the alien attack on Sixth Avenue, until mid-sentence the microphone went dead. And so the play continued.

Across America, many people listening to the play assumed it was the real thing. They panicked. Telephone switchboards were jammed. Terrified crowds mobbed police stations. People packed suitcases and jumped into their cars. They grabbed guns and patrolled the country-side looking for the aliens. It was chaos.

Meanwhile, in the radio theatre, Orson Welles interrupted the program to remind people it was only a play, but many people were no longer listening – they believed it was the real thing: the night aliens invaded America.

Race For Space

During World War II, the Soviets and Americans fought on the same side – they were allies. But almost before the war was over they started to argue about each other's politics. The arguments escalated. Within a few years, America and the USSR were at war again – against each other. They threatened to use nuclear bombs and stockpiled weapons, enough nuclear weapons to kill every man, woman and child twelve times over. But it wasn't a war of weapons. It was a cold war, a war of spies and propaganda, and a war of ideas and economics. Both sides believed that their system of government was the only right one.

From this cold war, the 'space race' began. It was the race to be the first into space, the first to put a man on the moon.

The USSR won the first race. In 1957 they launched the first artificial satellite into orbit around the earth. *Sputnik I* was about twice the size of a basketball and it carried only a radio transmitter.

Dogs in Space

A month later, the first living creature was launched into space, a little dog named Laika. She had been trained to be a cosmonaut, and during her seven days in Earth's orbit she was fed automatically from a machine. Unfortunately there was no way to bring the Sputniks safely back to Earth, and the little dog died in space. Her last meal contained poison.

The Soviet space program continued to use dogs in preparation for the first manned space flight. Three years later, the scientists worked out how to bring the Sputniks back to earth, and the two dogs in *Sputnik 5* were safely recovered. Belka (meaning Squirrel) and Strelka (Little Arrow) were the first living creatures to reach space and return to earth.

Verterok (Little Wind) and Ugolyok (Little Piece of Coal) broke the canine record for space flight when they orbited the earth for twenty-two days. Humans only broke this endurance record in 1974.

Other animals travelled with the Soviet space dogs – mice, rats and guinea pigs.

2700 BC
Chinese
make silk

Man in Space

Finally the Soviets launched the first man into orbit in 1961. Yuri Gagarin was the first soviet cosmonaut – the very first human being in space.

Cosmonaut? Astronaut? Remember this was all taking place during the cold war after World War II. A cosmonaut is the Soviet term for a person making flights in space, and astronaut the Western term.

Insects in Space

Over the past two decades, insect research has been conducted in space, in space stations such as Skylab. The common housefly is everywhere!

While flies that were bred in space (at zero gravity) developed normally, they didn't learn how to fly – preferring to just float around without beating their wings. Honeybees were unable to learn this trick, and they tumbled helplessly about in zero gravity.

The mutation rate increased for many insects – beetles, moths, fruit flies and stick insects – possibly because of the higher radiation levels in space. On Earth our

atmosphere filters out most of this cosmic radiation, but the insects aboard Skylab were not so lucky.

STONED SPIDERS

Scientists turned their attention to spiders. They were interested in (among other things) how spiders spin their webs under the influence of drugs.

Caffeine is one of the most common drugs consumed in soft drinks, coffee and tea. The spiders that were fed caffeine were incapable of spinning anything better than a few threads strung together at random. The drugs used in sleeping pills had much the same effect on spiders, they dropped off to sleep after they spun a few haphazard threads. Dosed with stimulants (benzedrine), the spiders were extremely busy, but their webs were riddled with holes, almost as if they couldn't concentrate on what they were doing. Similarly, the spiders given marijuana started off well, spinning almost normal webs, but they seemed to lose concentration about halfway through and lost interest.

NASA

The year after the Soviets successfully launched their Sputnik satellites, the American government set up NASA, the National Aeronautics and Space Administration.

After several successful space programs, NASA finally launched *Apollo II*, and in 1969 Neil Armstrong became the first man to walk on the moon.

In the early 1980s, NASA began its space shuttle pro-

2350 BC
*Great
pyramid of
Cheops is*

gram, flying the first reuseable manned spacecraft. The space shuttle is launched vertically into the air on a rocket. After take-off, the fuel rockets are discarded and the shuttle glides back to Earth to land on a runway like a conventional aircraft. The shuttle is used to launch satellites into orbit and to undertake scientific research and tests for the military. Military flights are normally secret.

Like everything else, occasionally there are accidents, and the space shuttle is no exception.

CHALLENGER

On 28 January 1986, the space shuttle *Challenger* exploded live on TV beamed around the world.

NASA had planned to launch fifteen missions during 1986. *Challenger* had successfully returned from its last mission just ten weeks previously. It was scheduled to be a busy year. And this flight mission was to be unique: the first ordinary citizen would fly in space. She was Christa McAuliffe, a thirty-seven year old teacher. Her proud parents were in the crowd at Cape Canaveral, Florida, to watch the launch.

The flight had already been postponed four times, and even though the weather at Cape Canaveral that morning was bitterly cold, the launch proceeded. Two hours after the astronauts boarded *Challenger*, they braced themselves for lift-off. Seventy-three seconds later, the stunned crowd on the ground watched as *Challenger* exploded into a fireball. Christa McAuliffe's parents also watched, horrified, unable to grasp what was happening.

Debris from the *Challenger* explosion plummeted into the sea sixteen kilometres below. Mission Control immediately ordered the sea and air rescue teams into action, but there would be no possibility of rescue. It was not until weeks later that NASA announced they had found the remains of the crew.

The space-flight program was suspended while the *Challenger* disaster was investigated. It was the extremely cold morning that sealed the fate of the *Challenger* crew. A small sealing ring (an O-ring) in the rocket-fuel system ruptured in the cold. It set off a series of explosions that finally ripped open the main hydrogen fuel tank. *Challenger* became a sky-born inferno.

In the final analysis, the *Challenger* disaster was blamed on human fallibility. NASA was extremely anxious to prove *Challenger*'s economic viability. The space program was being pressured to justify why it should continue to receive government funding. In turn, NASA pressured its suppliers to deliver to a tight deadline and keep their costs down. Corners were cut, warnings were ignored. The result was the loss of seven lives, and millions and millions of dollars worth of shuttlecraft, all for the sake of an O-ring that cost a few dollars.

WRATH OF THE GODS

FIRE FROM HEAVEN

Mary knew she would be late for church, but she poked the fire and set the kettle to boil over the flames. Her mother was sick.

'Are you sure you'll be all right?' Mary asked again. She was very worried about her mother. The physician didn't know what was wrong, though the last time he came to the single-roomed cottage he'd put leeches on the sick woman's back, allowing them to suck her blood. It hadn't seemed to help, but Mary remained hopeful.

Her mother sat propped up in her bed near the fire; she nodded weakly and pulled her woollen shawl around her shoulders.

'Go to church, Mary. Pray for me.' Her mother coughed again, an awful cough, but in spite of her pain she waved Mary away.

Mary would have liked to stay home with her mother, but perhaps the only thing she could do was pray. No one knew why some people got sick and not others. It was God's will. Perhaps this time Mary's prayers would be answered.

Quickly, Mary kissed her mother goodbye and took her

own shawl from the peg by the door. The weather was grey outside, but at least it wasn't raining. Luckily there was a stiff breeze blowing, and the smell from the open drain in the middle of the road wasn't too bad, even though the road was still muddy from the previous day's downpour. Mary lifted the hem of her dress and stepped over the puddles of filth. The village was almost deserted. Just about everyone would be at church. The church was the centre of village life, and the vicar was one of the most important people. He preached that people who didn't go to church were damned, and would end up in the fires of hell. Mary still believed that the sun and stars revolved in the sky above the flat earth. People got sick. It rained. The crops failed. People died. It was all a mystery under God's control.

Mary hurried, but she was not the only one running late. A carriage splashed past her, and she ducked away from the flying mud. That was the squire and his wife. They did not have to walk in the muddy street, and at the church they would sit in the front pew that was specially reserved for them. The shepherds and farm labourers who could not afford a change of clothes would line the back wall, and Mary would sit where she could squeeze in.

She was late, and the vicar was just about to deliver his sermon as Mary arrived. She covered her head with her shawl and slipped quietly inside the church, hoping no one would notice her lateness.

The congregation bowed their heads to pray.

Without warning, it grew very dark and Mary glanced around in surprise.

Outside the church's stained-glass windows the sky was black, and inside the air grew darker.

For an instant it was quiet, deathly still.

'Today we observe the Lord's Sabbath...' As the vicar cleared his throat the first murmur of alarm rose from the congregation. Here and there people crossed themselves and began to pray.

Suddenly, a deafening noise and the dreadful sound of howling wind filled the church. And from nowhere, a glowing ball of fire appeared inside the church. For a brief moment the spitting sphere hung high in the air above the pews, then it burst apart with a thunderous explosion. Mary was knocked to the ground.

In the front pew, the squire and his wife fell to their knees; the vicar was flung from the pulpit; bodies flew across the church, whirled about in the air before being dashed against the stone walls. Timber beams fell from the roof amid dust and rubble.

There were screams, and a horrible smell of burning as clothing caught fire, followed by more dreadful cries. A fierce wind raged through the church before the air began to fill with smoke and dust.

Mary closed her eyes and prayed.

The screaming and sobbing began.

'Help me!'

'Please, help me!'

Mary staggered to her knees. She was still alive, even though her back hurt dreadfully. The man next to her was not so lucky, his head was broken open and he was clearly dead.

Mary was too terrified to move. Surely it was the Devil sending fire and brimstone from Hell. Was it the end of the world? Mary prayed, convinced she was about to die.

1900 BC
Stonehenge
is built

But a little child cried, and Mary found the courage to feel her way through the dust and smoke towards the noise. A woman and her child were trapped beneath the rubble.

'Please,' the woman begged.

Mary found the strength to help shift the fallen stones and beams, but the woman's clothes were still smouldering, and she was terribly injured by the explosion. She would be lucky to survive. Miraculously, the child in the woman's arms was unhurt, and Mary carried him outside while others tended to his mother.

When the village counted the toll, fifty-six people were injured and four were dead, but, strangely, many people were completely unharmed even though they'd been thrown around the church. And there were more odd things: the coins in one man's purse had melted, even though the purse was untouched. Several people's skin was scorched beneath their unburnt clothing, while others had their clothes burnt from their bodies.

Later, Mary found out why her back was so painful. The back of her shawl and dress was burnt, and the skin underneath was blistered. For weeks the doctor dressed her burns and made her drink horrible concoctions. The vicar came to pray over her. But she did survive: Mary survived to hear the vicar preach that what had happened in the church was the wrath of God. For a long time afterwards, every Sunday the pews were filled to overflowing.

Everyone believed the vicar. It was the work of the Devil.

THE WIDCOMBE FIREBALL

What did happen to the villagers of Widcombe in England that Sunday morning in 1638? Almost certainly, it was ball lightning that devastated the church.

Ball lightning is one of the strangest phenomena known to science, and even today no one is able to provide a satisfactory scientific explanation. But there have been many sightings of ball lightning. During World War II, the crews of high-flying bombers reported balls of glowing light that appeared without warning inside their aircraft. Those crews that lived to tell the tale said that the almost solid balls of light would drift slowly down the centre of the plane before disappearing through the solid surface of the tail. Occasionally since then, there have been other accounts of balls of light appearing in civil aircraft.

There is a lot we don't know about ball lightning, but we do know that it appears as a glowing ball that moves freely through both the air and solid objects. Most ball lightning ranges in size from a centimetre or two to as much as a metre in diameter. It is usually associated with thunderstorms. People have reported ball lightning appearing as yellow, red or white, although a few people have seen purple or green glowing spheres. The spheres materialise without any warning, and sometimes emit sparks and rays.

Ball lightning glides silently through the air and can last for a minute or more before either disappearing or exploding with a loud bang.

Only one photograph of ball lighting exists – it was taken in Yorkshire in 1961, and is still the subject of scientific controversy. Taken with an open shutter at night, it shows a glowing trail in the sky above rooftops that disappears in a bright flash.

For a while, flying saucer enthusiasts claimed ball lightning was actually alien probes dispatched by mother ships orbiting the earth!

Some of the scientific explanations sound almost as fantastic. It has been suggested that thunderstorms might be so powerful they can produce highly charged particles (protons) which create in effect a mini nuclear explosion. Another theory suggests that lightning balls are actually minute particles of antimatter.

ANTIMATTER

In 1928, a British physicist suggested a substance called 'antimatter' should exist. He worked out a mathematical equation that proved electrons should have a counterpart with an opposite charge. It took a few more years before another scientist discovered the 'anti-electron' or the positron. Scientists can create them today in huge laboratories using a very, very expensive piece of equipment called a particle accelerator. The problem is, when matter and antimatter come into contact, both particles are annihilated in a massive release of energy.

The *Star Trek* ship *Enterprise* uses antimatter as fuel. Unfortunately, when Scottie starts up the ship's engines, chances are the ship and the crew would blow up. Of course, almost anything's possible in a science-fiction story, and one day in the future scientists may discover a way to use antimatter as fuel.

GODS OF THUNDERSTORMS

The people of Widcombe believed that lightning and thunder were events controlled by their Christian God. They were not the first people to hold such beliefs. Mankind has long tried to explain such a dramatic natural event as the thunderstorm.

Many ancient civilisations believed in thunder gods. Thursday is named after one of them – Thor, the Norse

(Scandinavian) god of thunder. Thor was renowned for his strength, and he was so strong, he became the protector of not only the gods, but also humanity. Thor carried a magic hammer to hurl at his enemies, and with the aid of magic iron gloves, the hammer always returned to his hands. The Norse people believed that thunder was the sound of Thor's chariot rolling through the clouds.

HUMAN SACRIFICE

Several ancient cultures made human sacrifices to their thunder gods. The Aztecs believed Tlaloc lived in a paradise. His servants were people who drowned or had been killed by lightning, and the clouds were his children. The Aztecs made human sacrifices to Tlaloc, ripping out the beating hearts from the sacrifices while they were still alive. The ancient Incas also sacrificed children to their god of thunder and lightning, Catequil. The Celts believed in two thunder gods, but only Tranis demanded human sacrifice (victims were usually burnt alive). Ancient Roman writers mention Tranis, and they associated him with their god of thunder, Jupiter. Jupiter was the ruler of all the other gods, and – most important to the Romans – he was the god of Rome itself.

The Japanese had eight thunder gods, among them Raiden, who had horns, a tusk and the features of a demon. He particularly liked to eat navels – so Japanese children were always dressed with their bellybuttons covered. In Chinese mythology, the thunder god was Lei Kung, an ugly, black, bat-winged demon with clawed feet, a monkey head and an eagle beak.

1450 BC
*Destruction
of Minoan
Crete*

Other thunder gods were more peaceful. North American tribes believed thunder was created by the sound of the mystical Thunderbird's wings. And in a lovely story from African mythology, Obumowas was not only the thunder god, but also the creator of all things. He made his home in the sky, only descending to Earth during the rainy season in the form of a fish-hawk, to court his earth-bound wife.

Thunderstorms and lightning are one of nature's most awe-inspiring displays, so it is no wonder people thought powerful supernatural forces were at work. Even today, a lightning strike is termed by insurance companies 'an act of God'.

ElectRic AiR

Thunderstorms are always dangerous. Recently, scientists have calculated that the potential energy of one thunderstorm can be the equivalent of several atomic bombs.

Thunderstorms are most likely to occur during the afternoons and evenings of sunny summer days. On warm humid days, tall clouds build up in the sky. As the sun warms the air, it rises, creating vertical air currents carrying water vapour. As the water vapour rises it begins to cool, forming tiny droplets that create clouds. But if approaching cool air gives the warm air current an extra upward thrust, the clouds rapidly become dark and heavy looking. These are cumulonimbus clouds, the clouds associated with thunderstorms.

Now comes the tricky bit. No one is absolutely sure how thunderstorms become electrically charged, but we do know that most thunderclouds are *negatively* charged at the base, and *positively* charged at the top. When the electrical potential between the cloud and the ground reaches a critical point, the air ionises (becomes electrically charged) along a narrow path which the lightning flash follows.

Each lightning flash is composed of several strokes travelling at about 1,500 kilometres per second (nearly half the speed of light), so quickly that it is impossible to see where it starts and ends. Generally, the lightning flash starts from the cloud base, but occasionally it originates from the ground. Lightning can strike up! Most lightning strikes occur within the cloud and only about forty per cent strike the ground.

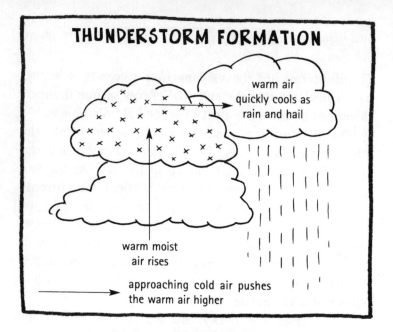

THUNDERSTORM FORMATION

warm air quickly cools as rain and hail

warm moist air rises

approaching cold air pushes the warm air higher

HOW CLOSE IS A THUNDERSTORM?

Thunder is simply the sound of the air vibrating out from the path of the lightning. The air around the lightning flash is superheated in a fraction of a second – so hot it explodes. The closer the lightning, the louder the thunder.

Light travels through air faster than sound, so we see the lightning before we hear the thunder. You can use this information to calculate how far away a thunderstorm is. Begin to count the seconds as soon as you see the lightning flash. The sound of thunder will travel about one kilometre every three seconds. If you can count to fifteen, the thunderstorm is about five kilometres away. Typically, thunder can be heard up to sixteen kilometres away from the storm – far enough away for you to enjoy the spectacular free fireworks display.

You might observe 'sheet' or 'heat' lightning, which is actually the reflection of an ordinary lightning flash against the clouds. You may even be lucky enough to see ball lightning!

ReD SPRiTeS anD BLUe JeTS

What you're most unlikely to see are red sprites and blue jets. Until recently, no one knew this type of lightning existed. It was only confirmed in 1994 when aircraft were flown very high above massive thunderstorms. Blue jets erupt from the top of thunderclouds to a height of about fifty kilometres. Red sprites are more mysterious still, appearing as massive but dull luminous red flashes directly above an active thunderstorm. Scientists are still investigating both types of lightning.

THeRe'S a LoT oF LiGHTninG ABoUT

Meteorologists calculate that in any one day there are some 1,800 thunderstorms around the world, with lightning strikes occurring at about 6,000 strokes a minute. The potential energy could supply all of the world's electrical needs!

Lightning produces a tremendous amount of energy. The temperature of the air near the strike is almost three times as hot as the surface of the sun. Even though three-

TRYING TO USE
LIGHTNING.

quarters of the energy is heat, the bolt may still have 125 megavolts of electricity. The average flash could light a 100-watt light bulb for more than ten years.

Until 1749, people had no idea lightning was electricity. An American scientist, Benjamin Franklin, demonstrated that lightning was actually a gigantic electrical spark when he attached a key to a kite and used it as a lightning conductor - effectively a lightning rod. He was lucky not to be killed. A Swedish scientist, Engelstand, was not so lucky. He tried to repeat Franklin's experiment, but was struck by the lightning and died.

LiGHTNING RODS

Have you ever noticed the funny-looking poles attached to the top of church steeples and tall buildings? Buildings can be protected from lightning by attaching a metallic lightning rod to the highest part of the roof, running down the outside of the building and extending into the ground. This attracts the lightning by forming an easy path for the charge to follow, preventing it from travelling through the building itself.

StRUCK BY LightninG

'he safest place to be during a thunderstorm is indoors,
'r inside a vehicle. Even if lightning strikes your car, you
are much safer inside a vehicle than out – safer still if you
don't touch any metal surfaces.

In Texas in 1979, three passengers were sitting in the
back of an open truck when it was struck by lightning.
They were killed instantly, but the three people inside the
truck's cabin were uninjured.

Don't use the telephone during an electrical storm.
Consider unplugging electrical appliances. Lightning
strikes can send a surge of electricity through the wires
capable of burning out every appliance that is plugged in.
If caught outdoors, don't shelter under trees. If the storm
is right overhead, the safest position is crouched down on
the balls of your feet. Keep the rest of your body off the
ground and your feet close together until the storm passes.
Don't play golf or wave things in the air (such as fishing
rods) as they can form lightning rods, providing an easy
pathway for the electrical charge to follow – through the

golf stick and your body. Stay away from water – it's a good electrical conductor. Lightning is not always associated with thunder. Remember the lightning flash comes first. If you're hit by lightning, you're unlikely to hear the thunder.

People who have been struck by lightning should be attended to immediately it is safe to do so. It might be necessary to apply mouth-to-mouth resuscitation until help arrives.

Burns are the most common form of injury. The extent of the injuries varies with the severity of the strike, how close you are to the strike, where the lightning hits you, what you are wearing, whereabouts you are, and other factors, perhaps including luck.

People have received severe internal and external burns from lightning strikes, while others have escaped with minor injuries such as burnt fingers and toes, or merely singed hair. One man in America claimed that his eyesight was restored after a bolt of lightning hit him!

Lightning DOES strike twice in the same place – photographic evidence proves tall buildings can be struck several times during the same storm. Rubber-soled shoes will NOT protect you from lightning.

LUCKiest MaN ALive?

Perhaps the world's foremost expert on being struck by lightning is an American park ranger, Ray Sullivan. He has been struck by lightning seven times, and lived to tell his story. He was first struck by lightning in 1942, when he lost a big toenail. In 1969 he was hit again: this time he lost an eyebrow. In 1970 his left shoulder was seared by a lightning strike. In 1972 and 1973 his hair caught fire after being struck again. His ankle was injured in 1976, and on the seventh strike his chest and stomach were burned.

Wisely, Mr Sullivan shifted into a house surrounded by lightning rods.

LiGHTNiNG is NoT ALL BaD

During a storm, lightning releases nitrogen from the air, which is carried to the ground by rain. Plants love nitrogen, and they grow especially well after thunderstorms. Although lightning ignites forest and bush fires, it probably provided primitive man with his first and most important source of fire.

Astronomers have also observed lightning on other planets, in the atmospheres of Venus, Jupiter and Saturn. Lightning flashes add to the spectacular display of volcanic eruptions. Huge bolts of lightning crackle through the volcanic ash clouds. The tiny ash and lava fragments rub against each other in the cloud, creating a huge build-up of static electricity until the atmosphere is supercharged.

St Elmo's Fire

The captain of a ship passing the volcanic island of Krakatoa on the night before it erupted saw not only lightning leaping in the clouds above the volcano. He also reported that the ship's rigging and yardarms were covered in pink flames and a dancing eerie light – St Elmo's fire.

Although St Elmo's fire is a relative of lightning, it is a harmless flame-like electrical discharge (not unlike static electricity). It occurs when electrical charges in the atmosphere build up around volcanoes, falling snow, thunderstorms, and even the tops of mountains. St Elmo's fire gives off a steady glow, but sometimes produces bizarre effects. In the Andes mountains in South America, strange streamers of light or a greenish glow reach high into the sky and can be seen for hundreds of kilometres. Meteorologists working in snowstorms have reported that their fingers become tipped with blue 'cold fire'. Completely painless, the fire gives off whispering or rushing noises. The effect vanishes when the electrically charged snowstorm passes.

753 BC
Foundation
of Rome

BEYOND THUNDERSTORMS

Thunderstorms are not always over once the lightning display has finished. Sometimes they bring hail and torrential rain, creating new problems. Severe storm weather and flash flooding can follow a thunderstorm.

True hailstones only fall at the beginning of thunderstorms, never when the ground temperature is below freezing. Hailstones are pellets of ice and snow. Remember that cumulonimbus cloud? Droplets of water or tiny particles of snow form in cumulonimbus clouds as they are swept up in the rising air currents. This rising air (or updraft) can also carry tiny droplets of supercooled water. This water is still liquid, even though it is colder than freezing point. As the supercooled water hits the tiny pellets of ice and snow, they instantly freeze, growing larger. The hailstones continue to grow as they repeatedly collide with more supercooled water and other hailstones. Finally the hail becomes too heavy to be held up by the air currents, and it falls to the ground.

Hail is usually less than one centimetre in diameter (large enough to hurt if you are caught in a hailstorm), but sometimes it grows larger still – much larger. In Bangladesh in 1986, the biggest hailstones ever recorded weighed up to a kilogram! Take cover immediately in any hailstorm and bring pets and animals inside to safety.

Hailstones damage crops, shredding plants beyond recognition and stripping trees and shrubs of their leaves. Hail can even kill. 1888 was a bad year for India. In the most deadly hailstorm ever recorded, 246 people died and more than 1,600 head of cattle, sheep and goats were killed. A hailstorm in China in 1932 killed 200 people.

STRANGE THINGS THAT HAVE FALLEN FROM THE SKY

In 1939 in Trowbridge, England, a shower of tiny frogs fell from the sky. While the fall only lasted for a few seconds, people gathered frogs by the bucket load. Tiny frogs also rained down in India in 1911. In Madras, a violent storm brought not only rain, but also thousands of little frogs – so many that people could not walk outside without stepping on them.

It rained crabs and periwinkles (small shellfish) in Worcester, England, in 1881. The seafood was reported to be quite fresh, and the local people gathered up the crabs and periwinkles in sacks and ate them. There was a shower of snails reported in 1886, and in 1892 in Indiana, USA, millions of brown worms dropped from the skies. A rain of sardines fell on the residents of Ipswich, Queensland, in 1989. It rained beans in Brazil in 1971, and unripe peaches in Louisiana in 1961. Luminous green snow fell in California in 1953. Little fish dropped from the sky in the Northern Territory in 1974.

Fish falls have occurred often enough that an official explanation has been developed. The theory goes that a

waterspout sucks up water and fish, carrying them for great distances before depositing them somewhere else as a shower of fish. This might also explain the frog falls. Who knows?

Other unexpected objects falling from the sky can be more easily explained.

In America in 1992, a family was disturbed while watching TV when something crashed through the roof of their living room. They rushed to see what had happened. To their surprise they discovered several chunks of greenish ice. As it melted it began to stink. The American Federal Aviation Administration investigated. The green balls of ice were actually frozen human excrement from a leaky sewerage system on an airliner. Unfortunately, such falls are not uncommon.

Something we might all dream about fell from the sky in Italy in 1976. It rained money when a light plane buzzed overhead, dropping bank notes on the startled but happy people below. No one ever found out what the motivation was for this benevolence. Other falls of money seemed to come from nowhere. A shower of ten-pound notes fell on Kidlington, Oxfordshire in 1995, and similarly, a cloudburst in France rained 1000-franc notes on the happy people. No one ever claimed the money as lost or stolen, it appeared to fall from a clear sky, and there were no tall buildings nearby where someone may have thrown the money out the window.

Perhaps the most unhappy and disturbing fall happened before the eyes of a woman in California in 1978. She was sitting in a parked car when a human body crashed through the windscreen. Luckily, she suffered only minor injuries. The body had been thrown from a mid-air aeroplane collision.

SPACE JUNK

Since man first began putting objects into orbit, they've been falling back to Earth. In 1979, an American satellite, Skylab, fell out of orbit, re-entering the atmosphere over the southern Indian Ocean and Western Australia. Fortunately the area is not densely populated and no one was hurt, but a reward was immediately offered and people hurried to find hunks of Skylab. The largest piece to reach land weighed over a tonne.

It's getting crowded up there. One American satellite was hit by over 200 pieces of orbiting litter and had to be repaired by space-shuttle astronauts.

HURRicanes and Cyclones

While thunderstorms can be dangerous on a local scale, the power of a hurricane can cause widespread destruction. As with thunderstorms, hurricanes are powered by warm moist air, and are accompanied by strong winds and rain. Hurricanes form over warm tropical oceans in areas of low-pressure air. They are fanned by high-velocity winds blowing in a circular direction around the 'eye of the storm', a relatively calm area of low pressure. Hurricane strength is rated on a scale of one to five. A Category 1 hurricane has winds of at least 200 kilometres per hour. A Category 5 (fortunately the rarest) has winds that exceed 250 kilometres per hour.

420 BC
First primary
schools in
Athens

WHaT'S THe DiFFeReNCe?

Hurricanes form to the north of the equator and spiral with a counter-clockwise motion. Cyclones form in the Southern Hemisphere, spiralling clockwise, but they describe the same deadly weather. The most spectacular photographs of hurricanes and cyclones have been taken from space, where they form huge majestic catherine-wheels of clouds. From the ground they are terrifying. The only protection against cyclones and hurricanes is early warnings and preparations.

CYCLoNe TRaCY

In the early hours of Christmas morning in December 1974, the people of Darwin in the Northern Territory had almost no warning a cyclone was about to hit when Cyclone Tracy altered course. A few weeks earlier, another cyclone had passed the city by. But not this cyclone. Cyclone Tracy demolished Darwin, with wind speeds of up to 300 kilometres per hour. The death toll reached 50, sixteen people were reported missing, and more than 30,000 people were evacuated. At dawn on Christmas Day, parts of Darwin looked as though they had been hit by an atomic bomb.

ToRNaDoes

The weather system has a few more tricks up its sleeve. In the right conditions, particularly fierce thunderstorms form 'supercells'. These are super thunderstorms, and they can spawn tornadoes.

Tornadoes are destructive vortexes of extremely strong winds. From a dark, heavy cumulonimbus cloud, a whirling funnel of cloud appears to grow down towards the ground. A tornado is born. The funnel expands rapidly, sucking up air from below, sweeping along the ground at up to eighty kilometres per hour. Tornadoes may last only a short time before the funnel withdraws back into the dark clouds, and then the danger is over for the moment.

The USA is the tornado capital of the world. Every year during spring and summer, the conditions are right for tornadoes to form over the plains from Nebraska to central Texas.

Weaker vortexes sometimes form over water, aptly named 'waterspouts'. They form beneath 'towering cumulus' clouds – tall thick clouds that do not appear to be electrically charged (they might produce rain, but not lightning or thunder). Weather vortexes also form over land and are called 'landspouts' but these never reach the destructive power of a tornado.

'Dust devils' are smaller air vortexes, not attached to clouds, which swirl upwards into clear air. Dust devils are most commonly found in deserts, forming when the ground temperature is much higher than the air above. The lighter hot air begins to rise in a whirling circle, carrying dust and sand with it. They are not usually dangerous.

A Final Weather Word

'Red sky at night – shepherd's delight.
Red sky at morning – sailor's warning.'
This is an old rhyme about weather prediction. Beautiful sunsets would invariably be followed by fine weather the

next day, so there was no need for the shepherd to worry about his flock of sheep. But spectacular sunrises often signalled bad weather, so sailors had better make themselves and their ships ready.

Why?

Dust particles carried upwards on warm air currents cause red sunsets. The angle of the sun's rays increases at sunset, and the dust particles 'scatter' the light, producing spectacular sunset colours. It is the warm air currents that promise fine weather. On the other hand, water droplets scattering the light of the rising sun create colourful sunrises, and if the air is moist in the morning, bad weather is on its way.

Unfortunately, the old rhyme no longer applies. Often, industrial pollution is now responsible for scattering the sunlight, creating the blood-red sunsets and sunrises of the twentieth century.

FiRE AND BRiM-STONE

LUCKY TO BE ALIVE?

Even though it was still early, Harviva was already awake. It had been hard to sleep through the noise last night; several times she'd woken and called to her mother.

'Sh, go back to sleep,' her mother had said. 'There's no need to worry. It's just the mountain snoring. Don't be frightened.'

Harviva did manage to get back to sleep, but she had nightmares.

Much of what had happened in the town lately was a waking nightmare. It all began a few months ago when the mountain rumbled and sent a puff of smoke into the air. Harviva had looked up from the shoreline and pointed.

'What's that?' she asked.

Her brother Stephen, who was three years older than her, had nodded his head knowingly. 'The old mountain often rumbles. Quick, it's your turn to take the tiller.'

Harviva was still uneasy, but she took the tiller and steered the little boat along the shore. Simone and Augusta were not far behind them and it was still a race. The friends often played pirates if they could steal an afternoon away from their chores.

51 BC
Cleopatra
is joint
ruler of
Egypt

A few weeks later, the truly horrible things started. A light rain of ashes fell almost continuously on the streets of the town. Within a few days the pretty little port town was grey and dirty, and Harviva's mother grumbled over the extra cleaning. Finally the mayor appointed a committee to investigate the mountain. Harviva wasn't interested, but her family was. Often her aunt would join them for supper, and then everybody argued about the upcoming report. Was the mountain dangerous? The committee reported it was not. The town breathed a sigh of relief, and Harviva's aunt baked a special tray of pastries for tea that night.

Her aunt owned a pastry shop on the tourist road winding its way up the mountain towards the old volcano. Many people stopped to buy a snack on the way back down. Harviva sometimes helped in the shop, and apart from playing pirates with her friends, it was her most favourite thing to do.

In the last few days she hadn't been allowed to go out at all. Mysteriously, hundreds and hundreds of snakes had invaded the town, deadly yellow and black vipers. Even their next-door neighbour had been bitten, and over fifty people died, as well as hundreds of goats, dogs, horses and chickens. Finally the Governor ordered the soldiers to shoot the snakes, and after several hours of continuous gunfire, most of the snakes were killed.

But today Harviva was anxious to forget about everything. Her mother had promised that this afternoon Harviva could go down to the wharf and play with her friends.

'Are you ready, Harviva?' her mother called from downstairs.

'Nearly.'

44 BC
Julius Caesar is murdered

To Harviva's surprise, when she got downstairs her mother was dressed for church. Harviva knew better than to argue. In the last few weeks, her mother had spent many hours in the cathedral praying. Although she didn't say so, Harviva suspected her mother did not agree with the mayor and his committee.

It was before breakfast when Harviva and her mother left for church. They were halfway to the cathedral when her mother suddenly stopped.

'Oh, no. I forgot I promised your aunt I'd mind the shop. Harviva, could you run up and tell her I'll come as soon as morning prayers are finished?'

Harviva nodded, glad of the chance to stretch her legs. She left her mother and headed up the road towards the mountain path. Even though it was a steep climb, Harviva was not puffed by the time she reached the tourist path beside the old crater. Her aunty's shop was not far away.

Suddenly, Harviva stopped dead in her tracks. Her skin prickled, hot and uncomfortable. A hot wind blew down the path, and long wisps of smoke trailed from the sides of the mountain.

Something was wrong.

As quickly as she could, Harviva ran to the top of the path and looked down into the old crater above the town. Curious, she watched two guides hurrying a woman tourist up the winding path from the bottom of the old crater. Behind them, little blue flames danced across a glowing red surface. Harviva didn't know what to think. She watched the tourist and the guides running as fast as their feet would carry them, when suddenly a puff of blue smoke rolled up from the crater, and they fell down as if dead. Harviva was mesmerised. Too terrified to move, she watched in horror. The glowing lava continued to rise in the crater until it covered the bodies of the tourist and her guides. There was no doubt they were dead.

Harviva screamed. She ran back down towards the town, screaming the whole way. Just as she reached the main street she looked back at the mountain, in time to see a river of lava flowing down the path directly towards her. In the town, people began to scream, running from their houses as they fled for their lives. Harviva also ran. Her skin was hot and itchy, and she noticed her hands and legs beneath her dress were red and sore. But there was no time to stop and think. She ran towards the wharf. The boat, the sea. She had to hide.

Luck was with her, her brother's little boat was moored next to the stone wharf, already rigged with its sail. No sign of her brother, but as she scrambled into the boat she looked back across the wharf. A figure was running towards her. It was her brother! She held the rope and waited, praying he would run faster.

'Run, Stephen, run!' she cried.

But the lava was faster still. Her brother screamed only once as the red river engulfed him and he was gone.

Harviva was too frightened to cry, too shocked. Somehow she untied the boat and pushed it away from the wharf, took the tiller and headed along the shore. Harviva knew where she was going – the little cave below the cliffs where she and her friends played pirates. Perhaps she would be safe inside the cave.

Nearly there. Harviva prayed. Please little boat, go faster, faster. Time for one last look. Instantly she wished she hadn't. The whole side of the mountain boiled down on the town. It was all gone. Everything was gone. Everybody was gone.

Harviva steered the boat inside the safety of the dark

AD 64
Rome
burns

cave and slumped against the tiller, exhausted, her skin burnt by the hot air. She was too terrified to think.

It was not over yet.

While Harviva could no longer see what was happening, she could hear. A tremendous hissing sound boomed in the cave as the lava reached the sea. In the cave the water surged, and choppy waves tossed Harviva, helpless in the boat. Quickly, the water level rose almost to the top of the cave. Harviva and her boat would be crushed. She closed her eyes. She was going to die.

Blackness. And then nothing. Harviva lapsed into unconsciousness.

Harviva dreamed, of playing pirates with her friends, of family dinners and happy, noisy streets. Somewhere through the darkness she heard voices.

'Miss? Are you all right, Miss?'

A man stood above her. A sailor. He lifted Harviva with his strong arms and passed her into others. Harviva saw her brother's little boat, broken and charred black above the waterline. Then she was aboard another boat, and the captain came to see her. He shook his head in wonder.

'Where's my mother?' Harviva asked.

'Did she live in St Pierre?' the Captain asked.

Harviva nodded.

He shook his head. 'St Pierre is gone. We found your boat drifting over four kilometres out to sea. Do you know how you got there?' the Captain asked.

Numbly, Harviva shook her head.

'You're a lucky girl,' he said. 'So far they have only found one other survivor.'

Harviva began to cry. Just at the moment she didn't feel all that lucky.

73
Masada
falls to the
Romas

79
Mt Vesuvius
erupts

BURIED ALIVE AT MT PELE

Harviva Da Ifrile was one of three survivors of the eruption of Mt Pele in 1903. The town of St Pierre, on the island of Martinique in the French Caribbean, was completely destroyed. Over 30,000 people died within a few minutes. Although Harviva was terribly burnt, she lived to tell her story.

One of the other survivors was a young shoemaker named Leon Compere-Leandre. He survived because his house was at the very edge of the path of the volcanic cloud. He also was terribly burned, watching in absolute terror as people dropped dead all around him. It was luck that saved him.

The other survivor was not found for several days, but he went on to become famous with the Barnum and Bailey Circus, re-creating his dramatic story as a circus act.

Auguste Ciparis was in jail when Mt Pele erupted. Fortunately for him, the cell was a concrete bunker with only one small window facing away from the volcanic eruption. Auguste was waiting for his breakfast when the air in his cell became incredibly hot. It only lasted for a few minutes and he held his breath (which probably saved his throat and lungs from being scorched). Strangely, although Auguste's skin was burnt, his clothing was not. There was a container of water in his cell, and, more amazing, it was still cool. For three days Auguste sat in his cell and wondered what had happened.

Would he be rescued or would his cell also become his grave? Finally, rescuers arrived and dug Auguste out of his cell. Auguste was pardoned and lived to become rich and famous.

Everything that happened to Harviva was true. Incredibly, although the Mt Pele volcano spewed ash clouds for weeks beforehand, the mayor reassured people it was safe. Not everyone believed him, and over 2,000 people left St Pierre, but unfortunately other people from outlying farms fled into the town.

St Pierre was a busy shipping port; its main cargo was sugarcane harvested from the plantations on the island. There were several ships at anchor in St Pierre. Only one, whose captain came from Naples (near Mt Vesuvius), decided to weigh anchor and sail out to sea. The port authorities threatened to fine him if he left before loading his cargo. The captain ignored them and sailed anyway. He said, 'I know nothing about Mt Pele, but if Vesuvius were looking the way your volcano looks this morning, I'd get out of Naples.' His ship was safely at sea when Mt Pele erupted.

Volcanic Bangs

Do all volcanoes erupt with such destructive force? Luckily, not all volcanoes are the same. The molten rock, or 'magma', beneath the earth's surface is in constant motion. Sometimes it finds cracks or weaknesses in the

117
Roman
Empire at
its zenith

rocky surface. When magma reaches the surface it is known as lava.

If the magma is very 'sticky', the lava behaves something like hot toffee. It oozes upwards slowly, building up a high, steep volcano on the surface. There is no immediate problem. But if the flow of magma is blocked (say, by solidified lava – a lava plug), the pressure builds up inside the volcano. The walls may bulge outwards. Gases are trapped inside, adding to the internal pressure. Sooner or later, something has to give, and this type of volcano can produce massive eruptions, including deadly clouds of super-hot poisonous gases.

Alternatively, if the magma is very liquid, it can escape through small cracks in the earth. The lava may spurt spectacularly into the air, but it does not explode, and the lava runs away to produce a broad sloping volcano such as those in Hawaii and Iceland. People generally have plenty of time to get out of the way with this type of eruption.

Silent But Deadly

Volcanic gases are extremely dangerous. Apart from their very high temperature, they also contain deadly chemical compounds; among them hydrogen sulphide which smells like rotten eggs, and hydrogen fluoride which is poisonous. And there are acid gases that burn on contact, eating away clothing, skin and lungs. But perhaps the most frightening gas is carbon dioxide. It has no smell, so there is no warning of its presence until it is too late. Carbon dioxide is also a heavy gas; it flows downhill and collects in low-lying areas.

The people living near Lake Nyos in Central Africa learnt about carbon dioxide's deadly properties in 1986. Lake Nyos is one of many small volcanic lakes in Cameroon, Central Africa. When a volcano lies dormant, the lava plug cools, and rainwater can collect in the volcanic cone. The lakes are not only beautiful, but also very deep. Occasionally gases from inside the old volcano bubble up through the water and flow over the surrounding countryside.

In August 1986, a small explosion in Lake Nyos released a deadly cloud of carbon dioxide. Nobody noticed. The next morning, 1,700 people who had lived in the villages below the lake were found dead. Herds of cattle lay like broken toys where they fell down. Birds toppled dead off their perches in the trees. They were all silently suffocated by the cloud of carbon dioxide released from the old volcano beneath Lake Nyos.

330
Capital of
Roman Empire
moved to
Byzantium

RinG OF FiRe

At any time there are about 850 active volcanoes around the world. Many of them lie deep beneath the oceans, and they are concentrated in areas where continental plate crashes against continental plate. More than half the world's volcanoes lie in the 'Ring of Fire' that circles the Pacific Ocean. Among them are Mt St Helens in North America, Krakatoa and Mt Pinatubo in Indonesia, and Mt Unzen in Japan.

Other volcanoes are extinct or dormant – that is, not presently active. But when volcanoes do blow up, it affects not only the people living close by, but the entire world, as the dust from the explosion circles high in the atmosphere. It's no wonder scientists are interested in volcanoes.

The soil around old volcanoes is particularly rich and good for growing things. Many mineral deposits are

found near old volcanoes. The intense heat from a volcano melts the metals in rocks, often leaving gold deposits when it cools and solidifies. The hot volcanic fluid also concentrates unusual chemical elements, and when these cool slowly, very slow crystallisation produces large, perfectly formed crystals. The hardest are diamonds: brilliant jewels created in the furnace of a volcano. Agate-lined geodes are another example of crystallisation born in volcanoes.

Pumice stone is created when chunks of hot magma cool quickly, while the magma is still full of volcanic gases. The stone sets like a hard, foamy sponge, and is light enough to float on water.

GODS OF FIRE

The ancient Greeks believed lava was actually sparks flying from the hammer and anvil of Hephaestus, the god of fire. Hephaestus was the son of Zeus, the chief of the gods, and Hera, his wife. Hephaestus worked in his blacksmith's forge deep inside a volcano. He was extremely strong and good at making magical objects, but he was also very unattractive, even ugly. He didn't live on Mt Olympus with the rest of the gods. One story says his mother thought he was so ugly she threw him off the mountain into the volcano, but another story blames his father, who threw him out after he tried to intervene in an argument between his parents. But Hephaestus eventually married Aphrodite, the ancient Greek goddess of love, the most beautiful and desirable of all the goddesses, though she was never a faithful wife, and caused him many headaches and problems.

As with just about everything, the Romans converted the Greek god to their own god of fire – Vulcan. He was a blacksmith who forged thunderbolts for Jupiter – the Roman Zeus – to throw.

Both the Greeks and the Romans sacrificed animals to their god of fire, but some ancient cultures demanded human sacrifice. In Nicaragua the most beautiful young women were thrown into a lava lake to appease the gods and stop the volcano from erupting.

Mt Fuji in Japan is still considered to be a sacred mountain. Legends say that only the pure of spirit can climb the beautiful snow-capped Mt Fuji. Every year, many thousands of Japanese still make the pilgrimage to climb the volcanic mountain.

VULCANOLOGISTS

Some people study volcanoes up close. They are called vulcanologists. Vulcanologists may spend years monitoring volcanoes, measuring the volcanic cone for any sign of pressure build-up or bulge. Dressed like spacemen in protective suits, vulcanologists take samples of lava and gas, and measure changes in temperature. They hope that one day they might be able to predict when a volcano will erupt. They don't always get it right. Occasionally, vulcanologists are blown up with the volcano they are studying. In 1991 in Japan, the husband and wife team of Maurice and Kati Kraft died when Mt Unzen erupted. On 3 June, lava sped down the mountainside at 160 kilometres per hour. Thirty-eight people were killed, among them the Krafts and a geologist and journalist studying the volcanic activity.

But perhaps the most famous vulcanologist was blown up with Mt St Helens in 1980; he was on the radio when it erupted, and his last words were recorded.

625
Mohammed
founds Islam

Death at Mt St Helens

Although the Native Americans said Mt St Helens was a fire mountain, the earliest European settlers had no reason to believe them. Mt St Helens was a tall majestic mountain, a beautiful backdrop to the alpine wilderness.

Over the years, Mt St Helens did occasionally puff out clouds of steam and ash, but it wasn't very impressive. It was not until the early 1970s that geologists studied and identified volcanoes in the remote Cascade Range in the state of Washington. In March 1980, a strong earthquake rocked the area and the scientists sat up and took notice. They converged on the area.

Within a few weeks it was obvious something was going to happen. The mountain's sides were bulging. The crater inside the volcano was changing. There were mud slides and ash falls. There were more earthquakes.

The local authorities began evacuations, but not everybody would leave. Teams of loggers continued to work in the forests, and enterprising locals were conducting volcano tours. Helicopters flew overhead. The owner of a local tourist lodge refused to budge. An elderly man, Harry Truman, stayed put with his sixteen cats. The mountain had rumbled before.

Meanwhile, the scientists continued to study Mt St Helens. By now, the vulcanologists were working in shifts, and soon it was David Johnson's turn. He was not the only person working on the mountain that morning: a photographer, Reid Blackburn, also hoped to take the photograph of a lifetime. He had parked his car close by, and intended to take his photographs and flee if the volcano erupted.

At 8:32 a.m. on 18 May, Mt St Helens began to rumble. A huge plume of black smoke and ash boiled up from the summit.

David Johnson was on the radio.

'Vancouver, Vancouver, this is it...' Then the radio went dead. No trace of David Johnson was ever found.

No trace of Harry Truman and his sixteen cats was ever found. His house lay under forty metres of ash and debris.

Reid Blackburn made it to his car before the eruption engulfed him. The windows were blown out, and his body was found in the driver's seat, buried up to the shoulders in ash.

Sixty people were killed. The most common cause of death was asphyxiation by ash. Two people died in a car travelling at 113 kilometres per hour. They were trying to out-race the ash cloud. Eruptions continued on and off for four days. When the dust settled, Mt St Helens was over 400 metres smaller. The blast flattened the forest for over 400 kilometres around. An avalanche of ash, steam and debris left deposits as thick as 200 metres in places. Trees, homes, bridges, even a logging station were wiped out. The wildlife did not escape. Thousands of deer and elk and hundreds of bears were killed. A thick grey cloud of ash covered the landscape.

HoW BiG IS a BanG?

Mt St Helens was not a particularly big volcanic eruption. It's difficult to compare volcanoes (all volcanoes are different), but scientists can estimate the amount of ash emitted into the atmosphere in cubic kilometres. A cubic kilometre would cover an area one kilometre by one kilometre to a depth of one kilometre. That's a lot of ash.

Mt St Helens is estimated to have sent one cubic kilometre into the air. The famous eruption of Mt Vesuvius in AD 79 was three times as large. A few days after Mt Unzen in Japan erupted in 1991 (killing the Krafts), Mt Pinatubo in the Philippines exploded. It sent seven cubic kilometres of ash high into the atmosphere, blocking out the sunlight near the volcano for days. Within a month, satellite pictures recorded that ash particles had spread around the entire world. While the authorities did have time to start evacuations near Mt Pinatubo, heavy rain fell after the eruption, and the thick layers of ash turned to mud. Hundreds of people were killed in devastating mudflows. It looked like a scene from science fiction, a grey world beneath a black sky. In the Philippines the eruption sounded like an atomic bomb.

BloWinG UP an IslanD

Although Mt Pinatubo was impressive as an explosion, over a century earlier another volcano erupted with such force that the sound wave travelled around the world.

When the island of Krakatoa in Indonesia erupted in

700
Chinese
war rockets
first used

1883, it sent eighteen cubic kilometres of dust into the atmosphere. Krakatoa was literally blown off the surface of the earth. The explosion triggered huge tidal waves (over thirty-five metres high) that swamped nearby islands. Over 36,000 people were killed and 165 villages were destroyed. The ash cloud circled the earth many times, and the global temperature was lowered by more than 1°C for the next year. For weeks, the sun appeared to be blue and green, and there were spectacular sunsets around the entire world for the next three years. When the dust cloud settled, the island of Krakatoa was all but gone.

Mt Tambora in Indonesia wasn't as loud as Krakatoa, but when it erupted in 1815, it sent eighty cubic kilometres of ash into the atmosphere, and more than 90,000 people were killed.

Death of a World

There is one other spectacular volcanic eruption recorded in history. Its eruption may have destroyed an entire civilisation in one mighty blow, leaving behind only legends and myths, and a few tantalising archaeological discoveries.

At the turn of the century, a very short-sighted man came to the island of Crete. One of his hobbies was archaeology. He was fascinated by strange markings scratched onto small ancient seals. These tiny seals were used as we might use our signature today. Hot wax (or wet clay) was dripped onto a document and the seal pressed in, leaving an individual mark – a signature. Seals were very important, and people were careful with them.

No one could explain the tiny marks to Arthur Evans. Certainly, no one could say whether the strange markings were even writing. It was an unknown language and a mystery.

Arthur Evans stayed in Crete for over twenty-five years and discovered the remnants of an ancient civilisation – the Minoan culture of Crete.

Dances With Bulls

Of course, the Minotaur is a well-known creature from ancient Greek myths, a fabulous monster – half-man, half-bull – kept inside a labyrinth. Was it just a legend?

When Arthur Evans excavated the foundations of a large building on Crete, he discovered a picture of young men and women somersaulting over the backs of bulls. Arthur also discovered a ceremonial room hung with bulls' horns, shields covered with hide, and vessels decorated with bulls. Arthur Evans believed he'd discovered the palace of Knossos, and

1066
Norman
conquest of
England

1096
First
Crusade

perhaps the legendary labyrinth, destroyed by an earthquake more than 3,000 years before – about the same time as the Minoan culture disappeared off the face of the earth. Maybe the legends contained a grain of truth. Who knows? But it's a wonderful story.

About 1450 BC, an island to the north of Crete was almost completely destroyed by a volcanic explosion. The Santorini volcano on the island of Thera erupted and then collapsed into the sea. Today, only remnants of the submerged volcanic crater are visible above the waves of the Mediterranean. It must have been one of the largest volcanic explosions in history. At least four times larger than Krakatoa, it created tidal waves almost 200 metres high (and estimated to travel at speeds up to 350 kilometres per hour).

ATLANTIS

Another legend comes to us from an ancient Greek philosopher, Plato. Around 370 BC, Plato wrote about an amazing civilisation that was destroyed 10,000 years before. It was the island continent of Atlantis, the home of a noble and sophisticated society that lived peacefully for centuries. The Atlanteans were famous for their beauty and high moral values. It was paradise.

Where was this fabulous land? Plato's description of Atlantis's location is unclear, but generally people place the island outside the Mediterranean, in the Atlantic ocean between Africa and North America.

1100
First university established in Europe

Plato is more definite about how Atlantis was destroyed. The people of Atlantis became greedy and arrogant; they invented powerful weapons and made war on their neighbours (including Athens). This angered the gods. Zeus punished them by destroying Atlantis with violent earthquakes and floods. In a single day and night, the island of Atlantis disappeared into the sea. Plato swore the tale of Atlantis was true. He read the story in old documents, which quoted their source as a reliable Egyptian priest.

Today, geologists assure us there is no trace of a sunken island continent in the Atlantic. And archaeologists are doubtful that a sophisticated civilisation existed 10,000 years before Plato wrote his stories.

But the Minoan culture was around 1,000 years before Plato. There are a lot of similarities between Atlantis and the Minoan culture. They were both fearless sailors and navigators; their cultures were peaceful and sophisticated; and both worshipped the image of a bull. Perhaps Plato got his sums wrong – remember he claimed his original source was Egyptian. There may have been problems with translation. Perhaps Plato also got Atlantis's location wrong by a factor of ten. Perhaps Atlantis was located in the Mediterranean, in which case the island of Thera and the mysterious Minoan culture start to sound a lot like the legendary Atlantis. Of course, Plato might have made it all up!

Death at Mt Vesuvius

Pompeii was a busy trading town of about 20,000 people located eight kilometres to the south-east of Mt Vesuvius, a dormant volcano. The main industry apart from farming in the rich volcanic soils was the production of fish sauce – a very salty, tangy flavour that was loved by the ancient Romans. Pompeii had fine public buildings and a forum (a kind of meeting place where business, politics and the law courts were conducted). There were over a hundred taverns and inns, as well as take-away food stalls and brothels.

The citizens of Pompeii were a rowdy, boisterous people. The town's arena (amphitheatre) could seat 20,000 people. Several years previously, fights had broken out at the arena, and dozens of people from neighbouring towns had been killed in the riot that followed. The good citizens of Pompeii were among the first football hooligans recorded in history.

But in AD 79, strange things were happening at Pompeii. The ground rumbled and shook, walls developed cracks, statues trembled and fell over, wells dried up overnight, and flocks of birds flew away. Even the animals were restless. Nobody connected these events to the mountain.

On 23 August, the wind blew towards Pompeii. Mt Vesuvius rumbled. Ash began to blow over the town, and soon showers of ash and pumice rained down. The citizens of Pompeii were alarmed, and many began to leave. But not all.

Early the next morning, Vesuvius erupted. A surge of hot gas and ash rushed down the mountain towards the town. People panicked. They hid or fled through the streets desperately looking for safety. But it was too late. There was no safe place in Pompeii. The boiling cloud cut them down, and they died choking, gasping for breath, suffocated by volcanic gases. During the day more surges of hot gas and ash rolled over Pompeii, burying the town and over 2,000 people under four metres of ash and pumice. It set like concrete over the town.

As time passed, the bodies rotted away, leaving hollows beneath the hardened ash. They lay there for centuries, undisturbed and unknown.

Occasionally a farmer would unearth coins or broken masonry in his fields, and eventually in the eighteenth century people began to dig around Pompeii, looking for ancient treasures. They hit pay dirt. But it was not until the late nineteenth century that an archaeologist, Guiseppe Fiorelli, discovered that if he poured wet plaster into the hollows created in the ash, he was left with life-like models of the bodies. Whole families lay together: a mother trying to protect her child; a Roman soldier still at

his post; dozens of gladiators chained together; even a dog still chained by its collar. Again and again, Fiorelli revealed and re-created the last terrible moments of Pompeii.

Herculaneum

It was a different story at Herculaneum. Herculaneum was a luxury seaside resort, nestled on the western slope of Mt Vesuvius. The winds blew away from Herculaneum. Although there was a warning shower of stone and pumice, the town was not suffocated by ash. At least people could see to make good their escape. But those who lingered to collect valuables, or took shelter in houses and cellars, were taken completely by surprise. Surges of hot gas and ash rushed down the

slopes of Mt Vesuvius at 110 kilometres per hour. The surges stripped off roofs and overturned ships in the bay. A glowing avalanche of fiery ash, hot mud and pumice quickly followed. Within hours, the people of Herculaneum were buried under twenty metres of volcanic debris. The first surge was so hot it charred any exposed wood, but the following boiling avalanche quickly sealed and preserved everything. Wooden objects were recovered from the town. They were singed and damaged, but they provide us with some of the only wooden artefacts from ancient Rome. Unlike Pompeii, there are no hollow mounds to be filled with wet plaster – all that is left are their skeletons.

Originally, very few skeletons were found at Herculaneum, and for centuries it was thought that most of the people escaped. But in the 1980s, hundreds of skeletons were found huddled together near the shoreline. Desperately, the people remaining in Herculaneum fled towards the safety of the beach. Perhaps they hoped they could escape by boat, but it was too late. Hot lumps of pumice rained down, and the sea was so wild it was impossible to launch anything. Some of them retreated to brick shelters near the shoreline; others were cut down on the beach.

THE RING LADY

In 1982, an American archaeologist, Dr Sara Bisel, was sent to examine the newly discovered skeletons at Herculaneum. What she found was to keep her busy for years. She examined several skeletons on the beach, among them the 'Ring Lady'. She was named after two

1920
First known reference to guns

beautiful jewelled golden rings which were still on fingers of her skeleton. It was an eerie sight. Beside ring lady's hipbones were two snake-headed bracelets pure gold, a pair of earrings and some coins. No doubt they were originally in a purse, but the fabric had long since rotted away. Sara Bisel examined the skeleton. The ring lady was about forty-five when she died, her teeth had no cavities, but she did have gum disease. She was a rich Roman matron.

Close by was a Roman soldier carrying carpenter's tools. He would have stood about 173 centimetres, and had six missing teeth, an old leg wound which probably caused him to limp, and a huge nose. Not far away, twelve skeletons were found huddled together for protection under an ancient brick arch: three men, four women and five children. A house key lay beside a young boy. A slave girl about fourteen years old cradled a baby in her arms. Dr Bisel reconstructed her face from the contours of her skull. She was pretty, but it was not her baby. With the little baby's skeleton lay a bronze cupid pin and tiny bells: only the rich could afford such jewellery. The pretty slave girl died trying to protect the baby. Her skeleton revealed what a hard life slaves lived. A week or two before she died, she'd had two teeth removed (there were no anaesthetics). She must still have been in great pain. Although she was well-nourished, her bones showed evidence she'd either been starved or very sick while she was a baby. And her young bones displayed the wear and tear of hard work, lifting weights that were too heavy for her growing skeleton.

Elsewhere in Herculaneum, a charred wooden cradle still contained the skeleton of a baby. A teenage boy lay in bed, obviously ill. Beside him were a woman's skeleton and a small weaving loom. A bowl full of chicken bones was on a small table. Did the woman tend the sick boy, feeding him chicken soup, weaving on the loom while she watched over him?

Back near the shoreline, skeletons were discovered in two more shelters, twenty-six in one shelter and forty in the other, including the entire skeleton of a horse. What were their last moments like? For a moment we are taken back in time, re-creating the desperate scene in AD 79 in ancient Herculaneum.

There is a sequel to the story of the ring lady's jewels. For nearly two thousand years they remained safely buried beside her. Less than ten years after they were dug up, two armed robbers stole over 250 valuable artefacts from Herculaneum, including the ring lady's jewels. They have never been recovered.

Poor Man

On the beach at Herculaneum, slave died beside soldier, rich beside poor. But in ancient Rome they would have lived very different lives.

Ordinary Romans lived in rooms behind or above shops. The living rooms were small and cramped, with low ceilings. Only very small windows faced the street (too small for burglars to fit through), and as glass was extremely expensive, wooden shutters covered the windows. Smoky oil lamps were the only form of lighting. The inside of poor Roman homes would have been dark and gloomy.

1453
Otoman Turks
capture
Constaninople

1453
Copernicus
publishes
his theory

Poorer residents rented rooms in large multistorey apartment blocks, up two or three flights of stairs, with no plumbing or kitchens. Water had to be carried upstairs, and wastes carted back down. It must have been disgusting at times. There was a law which set compensation for pedestrians hit by chamber pots emptied into the street. It was too dangerous for people to cook in the upper storeys of the apartment buildings, so they bought takeaway food and carried it back upstairs to eat. They ate bread, eggs, olives, cheese, vegetables, and on occasions meat and fish (if they could afford it). Their only sweet treat was honey, but that was a luxury item.

Rich Man

There were many beautiful houses and villas at Pompeii and Herculaneum. The rich Romans really knew how to live. Their homes were large and spacious, with many rooms and garden courtyards. They had running water and space for kitchens and food storage. They dined off silver dishes and drank from glass cups. There were beautiful dining rooms where they could recline on low couches to eat. Rich Romans ate lying down. They loved to hold parties and banquets, and each tried to outdo the other with exotic dishes of food. They served peacocks and larks, and even ostriches and flamingos. Of course, their ordinary meals would have been simpler.

Everything was washed down with wine or water. And Romans made themselves vomit between courses to make room for more food! Their houses were decorated

with beautiful
paintings and
statues, and their
gardens with fountains
and ponds.

ROMAN EATING DISORDERS

DOCTOR, I'M WORRIED ABOUT HER. SHE WONT VOMIT BETWEEN COURSES.

Everybody went to
the public baths; there
were three in Pompeii
alone. They were
luxurious, with steam
rooms, hot and cold
pools, massage
tables, snack bars,
and a gymnasium.

There was no soap, so Romans rubbed their skin with oil
or salt and scraped it off with a special tool to keep clean.
And everyone enjoyed the arena and theatres, even if the
ordinary people had to sit up the back.

SLaVeRY

Until Pompeii and Herculaneum were discovered, it was
difficult to work out exactly how slaves lived. Roman
writers of the time rarely mentioned them, and there were
only Roman laws and a few archaeological finds as clues.
But at Herculaneum, many hundreds of skeletons were
unearthed. The Roman people normally cremated their
dead, and for the first time archaeologists and forensic
scientists could examine a lot of ancient Roman bones.
The skeletons of rich people lay beside those of slaves.
Soldiers and children, babies and sick people were all
discovered at Herculaneum.

Generally the people of Herculaneum were well-nourished – at least they had enough to eat. But the skeletons of children as young as seven years old showed signs of deformity from working too hard and carrying heavy loads. Slaves in ancient Rome often worked so hard they were constantly in pain.

The might of the Roman Empire was not only built on military conquests, but also on the back of the slave. At one time, nearly half the population of Rome were slaves. They were vital to the Roman economy because they worked for nothing. And they could be bought and sold, bringing great wealth to their owners.

Who owned slaves? Just about everyone. Rich people might own anywhere between 500 and 4,000 slaves. Even

the poorest households normally owned a slave or two. Roman emperors may have owned as many as 20,000 slaves.

Where did all these slaves come from? Most of them were captured during wars – in fact slaves were the chief bounty of war. In one Roman victory, over 150,000 people were enslaved in one day. And at one time the busy shipping port of Delos handled up to 10,000 slaves daily!

Not all slaves were uneducated. Greek slaves in particular were often trained as teachers or doctors. Slaves also worked as artisans, making jewellery, pottery and clothing. They were used to farm the land, and worked as household slaves – fetching and carrying, cooking and cleaning. Slaves even worked as clerks and scribes, keeping records and copying manuscripts by hand.

REVOLTING SLAVES

Several times in Roman history the slaves did rebel. The most famous rebellion was led by Spartacus, who died over a century before Mt Vesuvius erupted. Spartacus had been a gladiator, and for two years he and his army of slaves defeated the Roman army. But Spartacus was trapped in Italy and there was no escape from the might of Rome. Eventually a new Roman general hunted down Spartacus, to the slopes of Mt Vesuvius, where he was finally defeated. Spartacus was killed in the battle. He did not live to see how his army of slaves was punished: the general lined the road to Rome with wooden crosses and crucified the remaining 6,000 rebels. Rome mercilessly crushed the slave rebellion.

1517
Coffee beans introduced into Europe

EYEWITNESS ACCOUNT

The eruption of Mt Vesuvius was watched by a young man who later wrote about what he saw, and what had happened. So not only do we have the archaeologists' stories, but also an eyewitness account.

Pliny the Younger (as he was known) was a seventeen-year-old student in 79 AD. He lived across the Bay of Naples in the town of Misenum. His uncle, Pliny the Elder, was with him at the time.

The people of Misenum saw Mt Vesuvius erupt. They watched as a dark mushroom-shaped cloud rose over twenty kilometres into the air. Lightning and flames crackled above Mt Vesuvius. The sky grew dark. Soon a rain of ash and pumice began to fall on the town. The people of Misenum were not only frightened for their own safety, they also knew something awful was happening on the other side of the bay. Pliny's uncle decided he had to try to mount a rescue, and he organised boats to head for Herculaneum. His nephew stayed behind and waited anxiously.

It soon proved useless to try to approach Herculaneum across the bay. The rain of pumice stones and ash, and the rumbling earth tremors, chopped the sea into terrifying waves. The boat could not even get close to Herculaneum, and Pliny's uncle directed it towards another small town, Stabiae, several kilometres south of Herculaneum. They managed to land, but the sea was too dangerous to return by boat. Pliny's uncle and his party took refuge for the night. It was dreadful. Stabiae was cut off. All night, ash and pumice rained down on the town. The people of Stabiae tied pillows on their heads to protect themselves against the rain of hot debris. The air smelt bad, and it was hard to breathe. At times the ash fall was so thick it threatened to bury them alive, and they worked all night clearing the ash just to survive.

At the height of the catastrophe, Pliny's uncle and his companions tried to escape in the boat, but the sea was too rough, and Pliny's uncle collapsed on the beach and died. The people of Stabiae were luckier: although the town was damaged beyond repair, somehow many of them survived.

Meanwhile, across the bay at Misenum, Pliny the Younger witnessed first-hand the deadly rain of pumice and stone. He wrote about what happened:

> 'To be heard were only the shrill cries of women, the wailing of children, the shouting of men. Some were calling to their parents, others to their children, others to their wives.'

Over many centuries, copies of the letter written by Pliny the Younger describing the eruption of Mt Vesuvius have survived. Only after recent eruptions have modern scientists realised his description was very accurate.

TOMORROW'S POMPEII

Several times over the centuries, towns and villages have been entombed by volcanic eruptions. The town of St Pierre in the French Caribbean forever contains the last moment of 8 May 1902.

1558
Elizabeth 1
is crowned

1559
Tobacco
introduced
to Europe

In 1985, another small city was encased by a volcanic mud flow. Armero in Colombia (South America) was devastated by the eruption of the snow-capped Ruiz volcano. Hot clouds of ash and pumice melted the snowfields, and a torrent of hot mud and debris roared towards Armero at sixty kilometres per hour. The city was destroyed. Over 22,000 people were buried alive. The hot avalanche set like concrete over Armero. There were few survivors, although rescue teams and helicopters quickly arrived to help. Only people trapped near the very edge of the flow were rescued.

Armero remains a snapshot of life, frozen forever in 1985. Perhaps, many centuries from now, archaeologists will dig at Armero and wonder how the people lived and died.

1605
Guy Fawkes
caught trying
to blow up
Parliament

1609
Telescope
invented

CHILDREN OF THE STARS

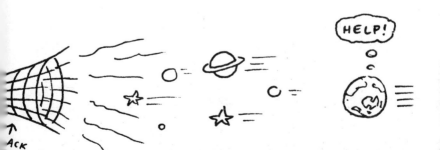

iN THE BEGiNNiNG...

In the beginning there was nothing.

An instant later an unimaginable explosion brought the universe into existence. The super-hot fireball of matter and energy expanded to create the fabric of time and space. Within moments, the fireball began to cool, and inside the fiery inferno, tiny particles formed. The universe cooled some more and the tiny particles began to stick together, creating the first atoms.

Time passed. As the universe cooled, massive clouds of dust and gas collected and collapsed, until finally they became hot enough to ignite, and the first stars burst into life. Inside the stars, new atoms formed, and when eventually the stars died in a massive explosion, heavier elements were created and regurgitated back into the universe to begin the cycle again. During the next few billion years, still more complex elements were cooked inside the furnace of the stars. Among them was carbon, an essential element for life – and the stage was set for the next great adventure.

In a corner of one spiral galaxy, a small yellow star was born, which would prove to be a very special star.

1610
Galileo
uses
telescope
on the
night sky

At first a swirling sea of dust and gas blanketed the star, but over time, lumpy planets emerged. The third planet from the star lay hidden behind a cloud of dust and vapour, its surface a molten sea of surging lava. From time to time there were catastrophes. Once, a smaller planet slammed into the molten world, and for an instant it looked like the planet would split apart and explode, but a huge chunk of molten rock and debris was blown into orbit, and the planet survived, claiming a satellite. Now the planet and its moon orbited the yellow star together.

As the fiery planet cooled, a thin, hard crust of rock formed on the surface. Volcanoes continued to spew molten lava and gases into the atmosphere, but eventually the dust clouds settled and sunlight warmed the surface of the planet. Water vapour condensed to form oceans. Lightning and thunder crackled in the atmosphere and huge landmasses drifted slowly across the currents of liquid magma. The continental plates collided, pushing huge mountain ranges high into the air and deep trenches back into the rocky surface.

In the oceans, a liquid brew of chemicals, washed from the rocks and atmosphere, surged back and forwards. Perhaps in a small warm pond, perhaps on a rocky shoreline, or perhaps even deep in the oceans beside volcanic vents, the chemicals linked themselves together. They made copies of themselves. About 400 million years ago, the very first signs of life emerged in the oceans. There was still a long way to go, but things looked promising.

At first the life forms were very simple, but as time passed some of them learned to turn sunlight, water and carbon dioxide into energy. Other organisms specialised in eating these life forms (and each other). But the ability to produce energy from sunlight was a huge advantage, and these organisms quickly multiplied and colonised the oceans, and, most importantly, they produced oxygen. The atmosphere began to change. As it did, life in the ocean continued to evolve – those organisms that converted sunlight evolved into plants, and the rest into animals.

Eventually the life forms became more complex. They grew leaves, eyes, mouths, fins. The oceans teemed with life, and it was time to colonise the land. Perhaps the first plants were washed ashore, or stranded in tiny ponds, but quickly the whole surface of the planet was covered in green. The animals followed, learning to breathe the atmosphere and live on dry land.

More time passed. The life forms became more and more complex, adapting and changing with the world, until eventually a gigantic race of animals evolved, and for 140 million years the dinosaur dominated the world. Small furry creatures occasionally scuttled out from the forest floor to snatch a meal – but they were insignificant beside the majesty of the dinosaur. Their time would come.

Sixty-five million years ago the planet had a date with another chunk of space debris. An enormous asteroid slammed into the planet, creating a cloud of dust and ashes that blocked out the sunlight and plunged the planet into darkness. It grew cold and the plants and animals struggled to survive.

Gradually the planet recovered, but the dinosaurs were finished. Now the little furry creatures competed fiercely with each other, and they evolved into many diverse species. The age of the mammal had arrived.

Many millions of years passed, but somewhere on a continent that straddled the planet's equator, the first primate stood up and looked across the land with intelligent eyes.

Perhaps less than half a million years ago, the first homo sapiens looked up at the stars. Maybe they wondered what the stars were, and how the world came to be, unaware that every atom of their world, every atom of their bodies, was created and born in the stars.

They, like all of us, are truly the children of the stars.

THE BIGGEST BANG OF ALL

Do we know what happened fifteen billion years ago when the universe was created? No, we don't. We weren't there. But this is what many of today's scientists think happened. It is called the big bang theory. Like much of this book, these events were re-created around what scientists think is most likely. As we learn more, they might prove to be right. Then again, they might prove to be wrong.

In 1965, scientists who believed in the big bang theory got very excited when it was discovered that the universe is bathed in heat radiation. The temperature of the cosmic background is about three degrees above absolute zero. That's really, really cold: at absolute zero even atoms stop working. But even so, scientists believe this is what's left of the big bang.

Are they right?

Only time will tell. In 1994, the big bang scientists struck a problem. Stars and galaxies that were older than the universe were discovered. How could this be? New theories have been put forward to suggest that perhaps there were multiple big bangs, or even parallel universes.

CREATION MYTHS

For thousands of years, ordinary people have tried to explain where the world came from. They made up stories. We call these stories creation myths.

The ancient Egyptians believed the world began when the sun-god, Ra, appeared above the waters of chaos. Each morning Ra battled with demons before he could sail his boat across the sky. Every evening he returned to the underworld for further battles with the dark gods.

Australian Aboriginal peoples tell stories from the Dreamtime, the time when the great spirits made the whole world – the land, plants, birds, trees, animals and people – and when the spirits instructed the people how to find food, perform ceremonies and live in the land.

The Bible tells the story of how God made the world in six days, and rested on the seventh day.

COSMOLOGY

More than two thousand years ago, Chinese philosophers called Taoists believed the universe was 'empty infinite space'. Before the sixteenth century, Western people believed the Earth was the centre of the universe. In 1543 a man called Copernicus published a book suggesting the earth orbited the sun. This was a revolutionary way of looking at the world. It was not until after 1900 that astronomers discovered even more distant galaxies beyond the Milky Way. The universe was bigger than we had ever imagined. Perhaps those ancient Taoist philosophers were right.

SEARCH FOR THE STARS

Copernicus's great work was not published until after his death, but within a few decades, a brilliant Italian scientist mounted glass lenses in a tube and invented the telescope. One fine night in 1609, Galileo Galilei stepped outside his house and pointed his telescope at the moon. What he saw changed the world forever. Galileo discovered the moon was not a glowing lamp, but another world complete with mountains and valleys.

Galileo turned his telescope towards the stars and planets. He discovered moons orbiting Jupiter, and rings around Saturn. Galileo wrote a book, and when it was published it created not only a sensation, but a lot of trouble for Galileo. At the time, the Church taught that the earth was the centre of the universe, and that the sun

orbited the earth. Galileo's book argued that Copernicus was right, that the earth did orbit the sun. Galileo was a brilliant but difficult and grumpy man. Eventually he was dragged before the Inquisition and charged with heresy. The punishment for heresy was to be burnt alive at the stake.

Galileo Recants

Wisely, during his trial Galileo recanted – saying that he was wrong and that the sun did revolve around the earth. Even though the Pope placed him under house arrest and told him to stop writing, Galileo retired to his farm and kept working. It took the Church over 300 years to review Galileo's case. In 1992, the Vatican finally admitted that it was wrong about Galileo.

1749
— First recorded
case of SHC

THE INQUISITION

The Inquisition was set up by the Catholic Church to investigate charges of heresy (not agreeing with the Church). But it wasn't until the mid-sixteenth century that the Inquisition got into full swing. Heretics were not the only people to interest the Inquisition; they were also torturing witches all over Europe, which presented some unique problems. A witch hunter in England developed a popular method of identifying witches. The suspected witch was thrown into a pond. If she floated, she was declared a witch and promptly executed. If she sank and drowned, she was innocent. Although men (and children and even animals) were also executed for witchcraft, women were the most commonly accused. Half the population of one village of 300 people were burnt to death over a five-year period. In one town in Germany, 757 people were burnt at the stake as witches – including children as young as three years old.

It was not until the beginning of the eighteenth century that sanity finally prevailed and the witch trials ended.

THROW ANOTHER WITCH ON THE FIRE, WOULD YOU DEAR.

Hit By a Meteorite

In 1978, scientists discovered a layer of a very rare element, iridium, in rocks that were sixty-five million years old. Below this layer dinosaur fossils were common, but above the layer there were no dinosaur fossils. Were the incidents connected?

Today, scientists think so. Iridium is a very rare metal that is normally only found in large quantities in meteors (or asteroids – meteors are just small chunks of an asteroid). If an asteroid were sufficiently large, the impact might create a nuclear winter effect, which may help explain the sudden demise of the dinosaur.

Are you likely to survive a meteorite strike? Of course, it depends on the size of the meteorite – but it has actually happened! There is a recorded case in the USA of a woman being hit by a tiny meteorite – it only left a few

1775
American
Revolution

1776
Australia
founded
as a
British
colony

bruises. Insurance companies occasionally hear about meteorites. Recently in the USA, a meteorite smashed into a man's parked car, causing extensive damage. A small meteorite smashed through the roof of a house and bounced off the furniture. And in Ontario (Canada) in 1995, firemen discovered a meteorite about three times the size of a football after they put out a fire in a caravan.

Yes, you can be hit by a meteorite and live! But take out insurance first.

SHooTiNG STaRS

Most shooting stars are meteors – space debris (usually rock or metal) that burns brightly as it enters the earth's atmosphere. If they reach the ground they are called meteorites. Very large fiery meteors are called fireballs. Generally, all meteors are believed to be the remnants of asteroids or comets, perhaps the result of collisions in deep space.

More than half a million meteors burn up in the earth's atmosphere every day. Most do not reach the ground, but occasionally some do. The largest known meteorite was discovered in south-west Africa in 1920; it probably fell to Earth in prehistoric times. Largely made of iron, it weighs over sixty tonnes and is three metres long and two and a half metres wide. Of course, if it hit you on the back of the head you would not live to tell the tale.

Other ancient meteors have gouged massive craters into the earth. The Barringer Meteor Crater in Arizona is over a kilometre across, and probably impacted over 50,000 years ago.

If a meteor is big enough, it is no longer a meteor but an asteroid – a minor planet. Many thousands of asteroids orbit the sun, particularly in the asteroid belt between the orbits of Mars and Jupiter. Where did the asteroid belt come from? We still aren't sure. Some scientists think it is debris left over from the formation of the solar system that never stuck together to form a planet. Others think it is the debris left from a planet that was destroyed.

Death of a Star

Just like people, stars are born, live for a while and then die. How long a star lives and what happens to it when it dies depends on a few things.

Remember, stars are born in massive clouds of dust and gas. When these particles stick together, eventually they become so large and heavy that their own gravity captures still more dust and gas. The cloud collapses under its own weight. It continues to contract, growing hotter and hotter. Finally it becomes so hot that hydrogen atoms smash together and form helium (the next biggest element). A lot of energy is released in this nuclear fusion reaction, some of which is radiated as light and heat – sunlight.

Stars come in different sizes. Our sun is a fairly ordinary star, not too large and not too small. If it had been too small it may not have been able to 'catch fire', and would never have been born as a star. Alternatively, large stars burn very fiercely and very quickly. They may last for only a few million years before they run out of fuel.

Our sun has been burning as a 'main sequence' star for four and a half billion years. The main sequence is the longest and most stable part of a star's life cycle. Our sun will remain stable for many billions of years to come, but one day it will run out of fuel – most of the hydrogen will have been converted to helium. About five billion years from now, the sun will expand until it is huge, and the outer layers will cool and change from yellow to red. It will become a red giant. Unfortunately the earth will be burnt to a cinder in the process, but eventually the sun will run low on fuel once again, and it will collapse to a tiny white star – bright but not very hot. By then it will be too late for the solar system, and only cold, dead planets will orbit the white dwarf.

1821
Electric motor
invented

TRAVELLING IN TIME

Light travels at a constant speed – 300,000 kilometres per second. It takes about eight minutes for the light from the sun to reach the earth – that's 150 million kilometres away. Distances between the stars are much larger, and scientists measure them in light years – that's how far light travels in one year. Work it out if you can: 9.5 million million kilometres.

The nearest star to the sun is more than four light years away. The most remote objects known to us (other galaxies) are billions of light years away. The light from the stars we see in the sky may have taken millions of years to reach us. When we look up at the night sky, we are looking not only into space, but also back in time.

Will mankind ever learn to travel in time? The physics and mathematics behind such a concept are mind-boggling. The universe is in constant motion. Six months ago the earth was on the other side of the sun. Not only does the earth revolve around the sun, but also the whole solar system is hurtling through space. Not only would we have to go back in time, but also space.

Consider the size of the fuel tanks on the space shuttle: most of what you see on the launch pad is fuel. The shuttle must travel at 11.2 kilometres per second to break free of Earth's gravity. This speed is called escape velocity. The amount of energy necessary to travel through time and space would be impossibly large.

And then there is the problem of paradoxes. A paradox is a problem that contradicts itself – it is unresolvable. Suppose you could travel back in time, back to before you were born. Suppose you prevented your parents from meeting. They don't fall in love, get married and have kids. You wouldn't be born. So you couldn't go back in time to ruin their relationship, could you?

supernovas

Stars that are much larger have a different fate in store. Heavy stars, ten or more times larger than the sun, do not collapse into white dwarfs: their collapse triggers a massive explosion, a supernova that marks the death of the star. For as little as a few days or weeks, the supernova explodes with the brightness of 100 million suns, hurling massive clouds of dust and gas far into space. Eventually, these particles will form part of collapsing clouds, and the process will begin again.

Of course, not everything is blasted away with the supernova. The particles that do not escape collapse into a neutron star. Neutron stars are very dense and very

1861
American Civil War begins

1865
American Civil War ends

1867
Alfred Nobel develops

small. One type of neutron star spins very rapidly – a pulsar. A pulsar in the Crab nebula spins thirty-three times a second! We know that pulsars exist because they emit radio waves. When these very regular and rapid radio pulses were first detected in 1967, people thought they might be aliens trying to contact Earth. But it only took a few months for the astronomers to announce the discovery of a new type of star – a pulsar.

BEYOND THE BLACK HOLE

For larger stars, a more exotic end is in sight. When a truly massive star collapses, its gravity is like a death grip, so powerful that all matter is crushed, nothing can escape – not even light. A black hole is created.

If you could get close enough to a black hole to switch on a torch, even the beam of light would be swallowed up. (Of course, by then the black hole would have crushed you and your torch to a mere smear of matter.) It is impossible to see black holes. So how do we know they are there? Because black holes affect objects in the space around them, so we can observe the effects even though we cannot see the black hole.

Of course, that's not the end of the question. What does happen to all that matter and energy crushed inside a black hole? It can't just disappear, can it? There's the problem of the conservation of energy. This is a fairly simple rule that says that while energy can be changed from one form into another, it cannot be created or destroyed. For example, when you turn on a light globe, the electrical energy is changed into light and heat energy. Of course, the electrical energy has already been changed from another source - perhaps solar energy or nuclear energy which has been stored as electrical energy. All so that you can turn on a light globe.

So, what happens to the matter and energy crushed inside a black hole? We don't know, but there have been some interesting speculations. Perhaps the matter inside a black hole is spurted into another part of the universe - perhaps even into a different time. Scientists scoffed at this idea, believing that anything approaching a black hole would be instantly crushed out of existence. But recently the theory has been revived. Perhaps it is possible to approach some black holes and use their massive gravity to accelerate a spacecraft to fantastic speeds. One day we might be able to use the warped space-time around the black hole to travel back into the past, or even to a parallel universe.

Sounds like science fiction? A hundred years ago travelling to the moon was science fiction.

1883
— Krakatoa
erupts

1888
— Most deadly
hailstorm ever
recorded in
India

UNSOLVED MYSTERY

In the early morning of 30 June 1908, a falling star flashed across western China. Hundreds of kilometres to the west, passengers on board the Trans-Siberian Express heard a roar overhead. They looked out the train windows in time to see a large glowing object race across the sky. For a moment they were puzzled. Then the entire northern sky lit up with a brilliant flash of light.

The train carriages were filled with curious and frightened passengers. What was that? They continued to peer at the sky.

A few minutes later the Trans-Siberian Express was shaken by a massive shock wave, and from below the horizon to the north, a huge column of smoke rose into the sky.

Closer to the explosion, a reindeer farmer raised his hands to his eyes, shielding them from the brilliant flash of light. Almost as quickly as it appeared, the light was replaced by darkness. A few minutes later, a massive explosion threw the farmer to the ground. The air was hot. The heat scorched the farmer's clothes, and the ground beneath him rolled like a wave.

The shock wave was registered on seismographs all over the world. For the next two nights the entire sky over Europe was lit up with a strange luminous glow.

Scientists were at a loss to explain what had happened. It was not until years later that stories of a cataclysmic explosion deep inside Siberia were reported.

1898
Pierre and Marie
Curie observe
radioactivity

Eventually a Russian scientist went to investigate. He was a meteorite specialist, and he expected to find a huge meteorite fall. But what he found was beyond his wildest imagination.

His first problem was finding a guide to take him to the area. The local tribesmen refused. They remembered the fireball sent by the gods over two decades ago. It was a warning from the heavens. Even though twenty years had passed, they were still frightened.

Finally the scientist bribed a tribesman to take him. They hiked into the remote wilderness. First they came to an area where the forest had been uprooted and levelled. In every direction the blackened pine trees lay in bizarre parallel patterns – all pointing away from the explosion. Some twelve kilometres from the edge of the destruction the forest was gone, totally incinerated over twenty years ago.

More bizarre still, when they finally reached the centre of the explosion, a forest of blackened upright trees still stood. It was an eerie sight. There was no sign of a meteorite crater, no sign of a meteorite.

For the next three decades, Europe was preoccupied with wars, and it was not until 1958 that the scientists returned. They were still unable to locate a meteorite.

Over the years several theories have been put forward. A comet disintegrated in the sky above Tunguska. An antimatter particle annihilated itself. An alien spaceship exploded. Or perhaps a tiny black hole collided with the earth, causing the explosion as it shot through the planet.

1903
Mt Pele
erupts

1903
First successful
aircraft flight

1905
Einstein's
Theory of
Relativity

1908
Tunguska
explosion

CARE FOR A LIGHT?

Some explosions almost defy explanation. Take the strange case of Spontaneous Human Combustion (SHC)...

In April 1749, some sailors passing a house early in the morning noticed a fire in a downstairs room. They broke in, only to discover a woman's body on fire in the living room. When they threw buckets of water on the burning body, it hissed and steamed as though it was red-hot. Witnesses described the scene afterwards. The living room and furniture were relatively intact, but the woman's body was burnt beyond recognition. Her feet, lower legs and stockings were untouched by the fire, as was part of her head. But the rest of her body was reduced to ashes.

An official inquest recorded the death as accidental. There was evidence the woman had been drinking gin earlier in the night, and she was smoking a pipe in the living room at the time. But the townspeople were unnerved by the strange death. They began to believe something more sinister must be involved – maybe even witchcraft.

Other cases are more difficult to explain. In 1986 it was reported that a Vienese pastor burst into flames and exploded in front of an entire congregation. A woman blew up on an operating table in Los Angeles, 1990.

Various scientific explanations have been put forward. The woman on the operating table was explained as a problem with the oxygen and anaesthetic

1914
— World War I begins

1917
Russian Revolution

1918
World War I ends

1919
Rutherford splits the atom

gas lines. Others have been attributed to the 'human candle' effect. In the right conditions a small fire may smoulder with intense heat for hours before it is detected. Effectively the fire is fuelled by the body's own fat.

One theory suggests chemical reactions inside the body may fuel SHC. Yet another theory speculates that SHC is a form of psychic suicide: the sudden release of psychic energy is responsible for the fire! Even ball lightning has been suggested as the culprit behind SHC.

Some cases of SHC may be explained by scientific investigation, others by urban legends, but others still seem to have no satisfactory explanation.

THE BIG CRUNCH

Scientists still look up at the sky and wonder about the future, and how the universe might end.

If the universe was born in a big bang, will it finish in a big crunch? Will the universe stop expanding one day and begin to fall back on itself in the final 'big crunch'? Or will it continue to expand, slowing down and growing colder? Will it become a freezing, lifeless universe? One day our sun will die, but perhaps before that, will we go the same way as the dinosaurs, destroyed by a massive meteorite on a collision course with planet Earth?

Good questions, but nobody knows the answer.

Many scientists are still working on questions about the origin and development of the universe – cosmology. Among them are physicists, mathematicians, geologists, biologists, astronomers and meteorologists (to name a few). None of these questions will be answered quickly. Many generations of scientists to come will also look up at the stars and wonder how it all came to be.

It's not just scientists who are interested in cosmology. Knowing *what* happened won't tell us anything about *why* it happened, so other people have joined the debate. Philosophers and writers, theologians and mystics – even ordinary people can join in.

Only time will tell. And we have a lot of time to think about it – many billions of years.

JUST IMAGINE...

It is the last perfect morning on Earth. Perhaps it's spring. You are standing on a hillside looking out across a valley. In the distance, you can see a river winding its way towards the distant ocean. Perhaps some ancient ruins are still standing, but they're overgrown with a tangle of vines and bushes. People have long since gone. Tall trees are growing in the weak sunshine and the sun hangs low in the sky. The spring air is warm. A herd of strange animals lumbers towards a waterhole near the river. But it's strangely silent, as though the animals and birds know something remarkable is about to happen.

You are the last person left alive.

Suddenly the sun seems to move in the sky. You look again. The sun flickers briefly, casting weird red shadows, and then silently expands. Within a few brief seconds the red sun fills the whole sky. There is only time for the herd of animals to pause and look up, only time for you to take one last look, before the sun engulfs everything.

In an instant it is all gone. The earth disappears into the expanding red giant sun.

1945
Atomic bomb
is dropped on
Hiroshima

1945
World War II
ends

1957
First space
satellite
launched

Later, much later, its fuel spent, the sun recedes, collapsing to a small white star. But the earth is gone; its oceans and atmosphere have boiled away. It is dead, as are all the inner planets, swallowed up in one

final

big

bang.

1961
*First man
in space*

1969
*First man on
the moon*

1974
*Cyclone Tracy
devastates
Darwin*

1979
Skylab falls out of orbit

1980
Mt St Helens erupts

1986
Space shuttle Challenger explodes

EXTEND YOURSELF

Any library holds racks and racks of books on particular topics. Go
and have a look.

IF YOU'D LIKE TO EXTEND YOURSELF YOU MIGHT LIKE TO TRY SOME OF THESE...

The Hinge Factor: How Chance and Stupidity Have Changed History,
    Erik Durschmied, Coronet Books
*The Year 1000: What Life Was Like at the Turn of the First
    Millennium*, Robert Lacy & Danny Danziger, Abacus
*Guns, Germs and Steel: A Short History of Everybody for the Last
    13,000 Years*, Jared Diamond, Vintage
A Criminal History of Mankind, Colin Wilson, Grafton
The Life and Death of A Druid Prince, Anne Ross & Don Robins,
    Rider

FOR SOME LISTS AND WEIRD INFORMATION...

The Ultimate Encyclopedia of Science Fiction, edited by David
    Pringle, The Book Company
The People's Almanac Presents: The 20th Century, David
    Wallechinsky, Aurum Press

THESE BOOKS ARE A BIT HARDER...

The Dancing Wu Li Masters: An Overview of the New Physics, Gary
    Zukav, Rider
The Mind of God, Paul Davies, Penguin
The Fifth Miracle: The Search for the Origin of Life, Paul Davies,
    Penguin
A Brief History of Time, Stephen W. Hawking, Bantam Press
Pythagoras' Trousers: God, Physics and the Gender Wars, Margaret
    Wertheim, Times Books

1992
*Vatican admits
it was wrong
about Galileo*

1995
*Chernobyl
nuclear
accident*

2000
*Publication of
Big Bangs*

SOME MORE WEIRD SCIENCE STUFF...

The Physics of Star Trek, Lawrence M. Krauss, Flamingo
The Science of the X-Files, Michael White, Legend Books
Paranormal People: The Famous, the Infamous and the Supernatural, Paul Chambers, Blandford Books
The X-Files: Book of the Unexplained, Vol.2, Jane Goldman, Simon & Schuster

IF YOU LIKE YOUR HISTORY AS STORY...

The Eagle of the Ninth, Rosemary Sutcliff, Oxford University Press
Restoration, Rose Tremain, Sceptre
River God, Wilbur Smith, Pan Books
I, Elizabeth: A Novel, Rosalind Miles, Pan Books
Roman Blood: A Mystery of Ancient Rome, Steven Saylor, Robinson Publishing
Venus in Copper, Lindsey Davis, Arrow Books
The First Man in Rome, Colleen McCullough, Guild Publishing

OR YOU MIGHT LIKE TO GET IN THE MOOD BY WATCHING A MOVIE...

Bill and Ted's Excellent Adventure (History can be fun)
Gladiator (For the might of Imperial Rome and fun and games in the Colosseum)
Spartacus (For the story of the slave rebellion in ancient Rome)
Ben Hur (For the chariot race in the Circus Maximus)
The Name of the Rose (A murder mystery set in a medieval monastery)
The Perfect Storm (See the little fishing boat go up and down during a true-life killer tempest)
Armageddon (For Bruce Willis saving the world from an asteroid impact)
Deep Impact (For the great special effects of the asteroid impact)
Dante's Peak (See a volcano blow up a small town)
Volcano (See the molten lava in downtown L.A.)
Twister (Tornado scientists get caught in a big one)

PHOTO CREDITS

ABOUT THE AUTHOR

Beverley MacDonald was born and raised in Victoria. Her paternal grandfather was an Anzac at Gallipoli and France; her father was a primary school teacher in regional Victoria. After the publication of her first novel she went back to school and completed a Diploma of Professional Writing & Editing at RMIT. She is a qualified editor, and currently works in children's television.

Beverley writes at the end of the kitchen table, and spends most of her time trying to keep order in a chaotic and noisy household.

ABOUT THE CARTOONIST

Andrew Weldon's cartoons have appeared in newspapers and magazines, on greeting cards and as tattoos. He has written and illustrated two children's books. He smells funny.

5 billion years
from now
*Sun becomes
red giant*